BEATING THE BLUES

"I realize that I will be sitting here writing 'do this' and 'do that' as if it were the easiest thing in the world. When you're down, you'll probably be sitting there at times thinking, 'If it were all that easy, who the hell would need her book?' In silent rebuttal, let me remind you that I know how hard it is! I've been there. You're right, it isn't easy, but it is possible. Once you make up your mind that you really want to get out of a depression, it becomes possible.

If, on the other hand, you really want your depressions, nobody will take them away from you. Not for the world! Nobody could.

There is always something to be depressed about.

You've got a choice . . ."

—THE AUTHOR

THE DOWN COMFORTER
How to Beat Depression and Pull Yourself Out of the Blues

JULIENE BERK
Foreword by Maurice Shilling, M.D.

AVON
PUBLISHERS OF BARD, CAMELOT, DISCUS AND FLARE BOOKS

AVON BOOKS
A division of
The Hearst Corporation
959 Eighth Avenue
New York, New York 10019

Copyright © 1980 by Juliene Berk
Published by arrangement with St. Martin's Press, Inc.
Library of Congress Catalog Card Number: 79-23223
ISBN: 0-380-55814-9

The St. Martin's Press, Inc. edition contains the following Library of Congress Cataloging in Publication Data:

Berk, Juliene.
  The down comforter.
  1. Depression, Mental. I. Title
RC537.B48   616.8′52

First Avon Printing, August, 1981

AVON TRADEMARK REG. U.S. PAT. OFF. AND IN
OTHER COUNTRIES, MARCA REGISTRADA, HECHO EN
U.S.A.

Printed in the U.S.A.

10   9   8   7   6   5   4   3   2   1

To my mother
for Hattye and Sidney

Contents

PART III
Preventing Your Depressions

What doesn't destroy me, strengthens me.

—NIETZSCHE

Foreword

In his classic work *Psychoanalytic Theory of Neurosis*, Otto Fenichel discusses Karl Abraham's discovery that "ambivalence is the basic characteristic of the mental life of the depressed patient, the influence of which appear to be much greater than in compulsion neurosis. The quantities of love and hate that co-exist are more nearly equal ... the patient is as ambivalent toward himself as he is towards objects. The sadism with which the depressed person attacks himself arises from the turning inward of a sadism originally directed outward."

In *The Down Comforter*, Juliene Berk shows a keen understanding of this depressive psychodynamic. Instinctively she knows that depression is anergic, apathetic, listless, and passive—the prototype victim stance. And so she sets out to encourage activity on the part of the reader: she suggests, entreats, seduces, demands, exhorts, strokes, berates, shares, communes, cheers, enlightens, and crusades for a rebirth of aliveness. Once she gets you moving, something will be set in motion; action and life will begin again.

Every psychotherapist knows that the depressed patient is an astute politician who wants your votes for his helplessness. This book can, however, break the tyranny of depression by giving the reader a measure of control: the reader holds the book in his hands, he has purchased the book of his own volition. He reads and uses the book at his own behest. In short, he animates the joyful spirit of the author, a relentless companion who then helps him to beat his depression and to stop playing the blues. By enabling the reader to have so much control, *The Down Comforter* offers him a unique advantage in his fight against depression.

Juliene Berk's personal approach, rich with folk idiom, universal themes, irresistible heartache and uplift, is grounded in a well-developed psychological sensibility. Her instructions emphasize decision, choice, responsibility, and tenacity—one must validate oneself. She knows that the core of emotional health is autonomy, that merely adding insight to injury is not sufficient. With finesse and an uncommon understanding of the absurdities, contradictions, and paradoxes of the human experience, Juliene Berk points out the wide range of human resources that can be used in the fight against depression. There are always options in life.

As is apparent, I thoroughly enjoyed *The Down Comforter*. It is a sophisticated, witty, insightful, therapeutic treatise on extricating oneself from the maelstrom of depression. The nostrums, insights, and sage advice of *The Down Comforter* can fuel a liftoff into nondepressive space; it is an excellent guide to solve and dissolve the depressive trap. There *is* a life after birth and our author has fought to live it and wants you to join her in the celebration of her victory and eventually yours.

Maurice Shilling, M.D.

Acknowledgments

In one sense, *The Down Comforter* itself is an acknowledgment of all the help, encouragement and support I have received from people over the years. To those friends whose stories, wisdom and humor are included, I give a special thanks for sharing with me what I have shared with my readers. In addition, I want to thank Dr. Maurice Shilling, Mary E. Woods, Dr. Joel Kovel, Penelope C. Marsh, Win Nadel, Nancy Allogiamento, Adrian Zackheim, and Diane Cleaver—each of whom, in different special ways, helped make this book possible.

Introduction

About a year or so ago, several of my closest friends and I were all suffering from downers at the same time. It seemed as if the whole world was in a depression. We talked frequently on the phone and exchanged suggestions —whatever had worked for one was passed along the grapevine to the other—and it helped!

It was then that I felt compelled to write this book. I wanted to reach out to others who share the problem of depression and try to offer that special kind of connection that comes from the insights, the understanding, the humor, and the comforting touch of someone who has been there and has dealt with it effectively.

It occurred to me that when you acquire knowledge of something on your own hide, it makes for a special kind of understanding—and through this can come a special kind of trust and a special link with other passengers in the same boat. Shared pain dissolves certain barriers and opens doors that might otherwise remain closed. This is what makes Alcoholics Anonymous and Weight Watchers work, and it is what enables cancer victims to help other cancer victims.

Some friends cautioned me that my book would get lost among the deluge of "expert" self-help books on the market. But after some investigation, I discovered that none of the available books about depression was written from the point of view of common experience. And since it was not my intention to replace professional help, or to substitute what I have to offer for anything else, it seemed to me there was a place for it. When you're feeling depressed, you'll take all the help you can get.

What is an "expert," anyway? And how do you get to be one?

The dictionary defines *expert* as "taught by use or experience; skillful; SYN. see proficient." According to that, I should have earned at least three Ph.D.s in handling depression by now—and I mean *earned*. I've been taught by much "use and experience":

I've lost a much-loved one through death.
I've lost jobs.
I've had a broken marriage.
I've been rejected by lovers.
I've had health concerns (three surgeries in one year alone).
I've known intense frustration in the delayed fulfillment of work goals.
I've had severe financial worries.

Significantly, after reading a portion of this book, two of my friends thought I had something especially valuable to offer *because* I am not a professional psychologist. These two friends are both psychotherapists.

In addition to the use and experience living has given me, I am a writer. Writers are notorious sufferers from depression. (Hemingway once said that all psychiatrists should take a crash course in short-story writing in order to learn something about depression. I think what he had in mind was the special advantage of the "tattoo-tutelage" that writers receive on their skins.) Perhaps the writer's susceptibility to depression has to do with the fact that what she writes is an extension of herself—like octopus arms (or legs). She can't sit on her tentacles. She can't hide them. She can't even sheath them in protective armor. She's just got to let them all hang out and swim around, risking.

Grappling, coping, struggling, wrestling, fighting depression has strengthened me. If it hadn't, I'd be dead by now. But my battles aren't over. I have to win them again and again. I become a more seasoned warrior as the battles continue. Perhaps I win a given battle more quickly now than I might have once. Perhaps I can negotiate my way out of one that might have overtaken me in the past—but battles with depression are seldom won once and for all. The struggle is constant, just as life being lived is constant. We can hope to become stronger as we learn more about ourselves, and we can hope to teach ourselves to be more artful dodgers. We can also find salves that will help us heal more quickly when we "take one" on the heart.

There *is* help. Diversified, specific, and general. Help from many different sources couched in many different terms. (You will find a section in the Appendix describing different kinds of therapy.) The important thing is to find help worded in a way that gets through to *you*, from people *you* will listen to. We've all had the experience of receiving the same advice or suggestions ten, twenty, thirty, or a thousand times—and for some reason, it didn't get through. How many times have you been told something about yourself that you might acknowledge as being true or worthwhile and *still* you dismissed it because you weren't ready to listen? For that matter, how many times have you told yourself what you should be doing (or not doing) for your own good, and not been ready to heed that either? Anyone who has given up smoking, for instance, will tell you that before anything works, you have to be *ready*. Being ready is half the battle, but the right words at the right moment make the magic that does the trick. That's the moment when all of a sudden someone rephrases the same thing you've heard over and over—and *bingo*, it comes through loud and clear.

A friend of mine who's had a weight problem for years thought she had heard everything there was to hear on the subject. Then recently another friend suggested that it is possible to be both attractive *and* intelligent at the same time. Suddenly she realized that all through her life, she had been thinking that she had to choose one or the other. The idea of being able to handle being both had never even occurred to her. She had therefore spent her life concentrating on being intelligent. Finally, when she felt sufficiently confident in that area, she was ready to have those words get through to her. Why had such a simple thought never gotten through before? There could be many explanations: she may not have felt the special trust which made her listen to this particular friend; the wording of the message may not have been right; she may not have been free of other blocking concerns, as I mentioned before; or it may have been a combination of factors. Whatever the reasons, she had not been ready until that moment. She has already lost twenty-eight pounds in six weeks!

We are all aware of how words can be interpreted in an almost infinite variety of ways—how each reader or listener brings his or her own meaning to what is being said; how within a meaning, many shades and nuances may be present but not accounted for; how we continuously strive to communicate what we feel and think with varying degrees of success.

A very great and famous singing teacher I once knew said he could tell a student everything he knew about singing in one hour. The rest was repetition. People studied with him for years, listening to him repeat his lessons and going home to practice what he advised. They learned by feeling it work on their own hides. Once you find something that works for you, repetition is the tool that engraves the lesson indelibly on your mind. My friend who lost the twenty-eight pounds will have to repeat the lesson she learned that day over and over if she wants to keep on losing weight.

Perhaps, out of my experience, I can say something in *my* words that will dissolve the barrier and open the door —and you may be able to try something I suggest and have it work for you on your own hide. The engraving part is up to you.

I like to think of this book as a collection of nostrums, because a nostrum is a medicine recommended by its preparer. Some of my nostrums are in the form of lists of things to try; some are in the form of ideas to think about; and some are in the form of stories. My suggestions may frequently seem unconventional—to say the least. You may also notice a slight irreverence in my tone: plain talk can be very effective. I figure that the tough-minded approach —looking at what really happens and being willing to try

20

whatever works—is exactly what is needed or maybe you wouldn't be so depressed in the first place. It's us sensitive, deep-feeling types who tend to suffer from what I like to call the idealist's disease. All too often it's *toughness* we need the most and want the least.

These are a few general points I want to make:

1. Depression hits in varying degrees of intensity at various times, and will yield to or resist your efforts accordingly. I have scaled my nostrums in many instances to match the different degrees, so you must seek out those that seem to you to be the correct dosage at a given time. You may also have to do a bit of experimenting up and down the scale to find the right tone at the right time. The most intense degree of depression is an extremely serious condition which can even call for hospitalization. Don't fool around if you're too despairing to try anything. No book can help then. First seek some good, solid professional help and then come back to books. A book can *help prevent* someone from getting that low. There is help for all degrees of depression: self-help, help from a mate or a lover, help from a friend, help from a book, professional counseling . . . all of which can make a difference in mitigating the severity or duration of your downer.

I am addressing those of you who are reaching out for help, even if only to a bookshelf at this point. There are times when a book can tide you over till your next appointment with your shrink. There are times when a book can actually help you get through a bad patch all by yourself. There are times when a book can help you help someone else. And there are times when a book can help you face the fact that needing outside help is not so terrible as you may have thought.

I've had lots of help in my life, professional and otherwise. I'm grateful for it, and I'm hopeful that I will be able to give back some small measure of what I have received. Most of us are not in the absolute pits most of the time. Ground zero is beyond my reach, and I don't want to pretend otherwise. So if you find that you are too low even to finish reading this book, put it aside and get some individual, professional attention. Later on, you'll be able to come back and pick up where we left off.

2. You may or may not be a writer or an artist. You may or may not have a life's work or a career. You may be a man or a woman. You may be married or single, with children or childless. You may be young, old, or middle-aged. The differences evaporate when one human being looks at the life experience of another human being—particularly when both of them have suffered from the same condition. The person who has a career can experience the same agony of inadequacy as someone who has not— sometimes the greatest success story hides the real story of the depression that results from overwhelming feelings of inadequacy and unworthiness. It is easy to ascribe feelings of inadequacy to a lack of a career or satisfying work. But the truth of the matter is that feeling inadequate is a coin with two sides: you can feel unworthy and inadequate and therefore not go out to seek the very work you believe would make you feel good about yourself if only you had it. Alternatively, you can have the work but withhold from yourself the pleasure and enjoyment of feeling good about it because you don't feel worthy. Two sides of the same coin is what I call a close relationship.

It is important for people with different life-styles and life experiences to see that they share the essential problems, are alike in the essential ways, and can learn from each other about means of coping. A writer or an artist can help a nonartist find creative ways of looking at or dealing with problems. A person who is not a writer or an artist can help the artist see that basic humanity is the stuff of which art is made. A man can relate to a woman's feeling of not "doing enough" with her life, and a woman can relate to the fact that a man's job is often invested with gratifications that shore up his ego. We all have a great deal to say to one another if we are ready to look for and listen to the similarities among us rather than the differences.

If you get into the habit of seeking the similarities rather than the differences, you will find that you relate more easily to others. Have you ever noticed how some people constantly attempt to establish that they are different from you rather than like you? This is a means of creating instant distance automatically. Perhaps this kind of distancing is an unconscious habit of yours. If so, do you suffer from a feeling of loneliness? The two go together. Those who create distance also create loneliness and alienation. I will be discussing loneliness later on in a chapter all to itself. For the moment, remember that loneliness is an important adjunct to depression—but not, in itself, a cause.

3. Although I firmly believe that similarities are more important than differences, differences can be very instructive if you scrutinize them. Statistical reports tell us that more women than men suffer from depression. Is this true? I would have to say that in my experience it appears to be true. Why should this be so? I think there are several reasons: Until the women's movement, it was usually only the man with artistic sensibilities who went in for self-examination —not the average man—so relatively few men faced up to whatever depressed feelings they may have had; feelings of depression were not considered "manly" in our society, and again, we owe women's lib a vote of thanks for freeing both sexes to be themselves and admit their feelings; traditionally, men are an active lot—their days are filled with trying to earn a living and get ahead, and their free time is often spent in either watching or participating in active interests; they have not had the time or incentive for self-examination. I am, of course, making one of those clumsy generalizations that can be shot down at any bend in the road, yet there is something to learn from it. It boils down to two factors: a) men have in the past spent less time thinking about themselves, and b) men have traditionally been more active than women. As you read

23

the book, you will see why and how these two factors have made such a *difference* and why, in the past, men appear to have suffered less from depression. All that is changing. Men are facing their inner feelings more than they used to. Women are more involved in active pursuits. As this happens, the similarities increase, the common human link between the sexes grows stronger and the artificially distancing factors recede. There are many reasons why there is more depression than ever among both sexes—but the facing of it by both men and women cannot help but be better than running away.

4. I have structured this book so that there is a kind of building process—a building toward understanding. What I have to say will carry more weight, have more meaning, be more significant if you arrive at it when you are ready. I have tried to say the right words at the right time and in the right place. This is why, for example, I have saved How to Use This Book for the final chapter instead of placing it up front. It will only have real significance after you've read everything else that comes first.

5. If you live with an adult, try to get him or her or them to read this book if you find it helpful. My words, printed and aimed at "to whom it may concern," may get through where yours have been blocked. It is hard to live with a depressive, especially when the depressive doesn't feel up to talking about it. Perhaps your live-in companion or companions will be able to look at you and relate to your problems in a new way.

6. Even if one of my nostrums works once, it may not *always* work. Nothing *always* works. I am a great believer in variety—if this doesn't work, try that; then come back and try this next time. Therefore, I am offering a whole range of nostrums in the hope that there will always be at least one that will help at any given moment. Some people will find certain things that work more or less consistently for them. Fine! Stick with what works! And if ever it doesn't, let there be a whole bag of nostrums to draw from— in case, and in reserve.

Very often, because depression hinges on a complex and delicate *balance* of factors within the individual, the balance can be tipped in either direction (toward feeling better or toward feeling worse) by a small change. Merely having something to try can affect the balance—just knowing that someone else has felt as down as you do at this moment and has gotten up again can turn the tide toward feeling better.

I realize that I will be sitting here writing "do this" and "do that" as if it were the easiest thing in the world. When you're down, you'll probably be sitting there at times thinking, "If it were all that easy, who the hell would need her book?" In silent rebuttal, let me remind you that I know how hard it is! I've been there. You're right, it isn't easy, but it is possible. Once you make up your mind that you really want to get out of a depression, it becomes possible.

If, on the other hand, you really want your depressions, nobody will take them away from you. Not for the world! Nobody could. You can feel good and depressed because you bought this book and it isn't going to help. You've been had again.

There is always something to be depressed about.

You've got a choice about whether you give in to it. If you do give in to it habitually—if you wrap yourself up in it and hug it to you—then ask yourself if you're using your depressions to get off on feeling down. If so, why not try wrapping yourself up in *The Down Comforter* instead?

If you want to get rid of your depression, I hope you'll give my nostrums a try.

PART I

Getting to Know
Your Depressions

Analyzing the Reasons for and/or the Causes of Your Depressions or You Can't Tell a Tiger by Its Spots

As I see it, there are four basic reasons for and/or causes of your depressions. Four types. I call them:

1. circumstantial
2. chemical or barometric
3. entertainment
4. habitual

It's likely that you have experienced all four at different times, so the first step in getting to know your depressions is to figure out *which one* you're having *each time* you have one. They're not all alike, you know—far from it. So for pity's sake, don't take on all black pits at once, which is what happens if you fail to distinguish *this particular one* from any other. If you hear yourself saying, "Oh God, I'm in a depression again"—watch out! "A" depression is so vague that it forces you to take on ALL depression. Besides which, when it comes time to select an appropriate nostrum, you have to know which type you're dealing with. There's no sense in using mouth-to-mouth resuscitation on yourself if you're choking to death on a bone.

How *do* you distinguish *this depression* from all other depressions?

Circumstantial depression is the one nearly everyone suffers from at some point in life, although many people may not describe it as depression. Circumstantial simply means when circumstances dump a load of crap in your lap. Such as: after working for the same company for twenty-two years, it goes bankrupt and you lose your job and pension. Circumstantial is what you are a mere victim of, through no fault of your own. That sounds straightforward enough, except that since this is the kind of depression which we feel is the most honorable, we tend to get sloppy sometimes and assign other types to this category.

And by the way, we *do* put value judgments on the various kinds of depression. Circumstantial is the most noble of them all, so naturally, whenever we can, we like to throw our downer in that direction. But what if it isn't really circumstantial? Then we're thinking about it in the wrong way, and if this is the case, we're doomed to wallow around in it until it wears itself out. Therefore, before you drop your blues in the victim basket, you have to check it out and make sure it's a bona fide, genuine-type circumstantial depression—and make sure that it doesn't truly belong in one of the other three categories.

Let's say that at first glance, it looks circumstantial—the company is folding and leaving you out on the street at age forty-four. Just to be sure, check it out by asking yourself the following questions:

1. Did I personally run the business into the ground?
2. Is it my fault that Japanese technology turns out far better and far cheaper kichibuzus than my company did?
3. Can I help it if they are now making cigarette boxes out of plastic instead of mother-of-pearl?

Naturally, these are only sample questions—but you'll be able to substitute appropriate ones for your particular situation. In so doing, you will have to think about yourself vis-à-vis this particular situation. Don't be too anxious to say yes or no—but if you can honestly answer no to all the questions you pose for yourself, chances are good that you are *not* to blame for your company's demise, your job loss, and the resultant depression. Good. You can put that one neatly into the circumstantial basket and then begin to deal with it as pure and simple bad breaks and rotten luck, without mixing it all up with self-blame and running yourself into the ground for being inadequate and self-destructive and causing your own bad fortune. You can clear your channels for the action that's coming with an honest appraisal: "I'm okay. Damn it! I did a very good job for twenty-two years and another company will be damned glad to get a grand person like me!" Expletives help clear the channels, so use ones that are strong enough to do the trick.

Step one is accomplished—you have determined that you are in a circumstantial depression. Now you can proceed to consider the nostrums for dealing with this type. That comes in Part Two of the book.

Back to types.

Chemical or *barometric* depression is the one that has a lot to do with fluids . . . or liquids (Somebody once told me the difference but I can't recall what it is.) There is a wide range of possible causes for a chemical depression: everything from the common cold to a serious imbalance in your body chemistry. Beginning with the least serious and most temporary types, you can blame things like trace chemicals, germ bugs, and other minuscule factors that swim around inside you, for creating all sorts of interesting and obscure effects on your psyche. Actually not much is known about the more elusive of these little devils and how they wreak their havoc, so be very wary about assigning your blues to arcane antigens at war within your bloodstream. They indeed may be—but on the other hand, it could simply be a cold coming on, or perhaps you're incubating chicken pox. It could even be that the antibiotics or medication you took to get rid of the bugs is causing your chemical streak of the blues. For all you know, you might even have something tricky like hypoglycemia. So when you feel rotten and you don't know why—but you *do* know that whatever it is is making you feel mean and depressed —check it out with your physician. The main point is not to make any half-baked allegations about the actual causes of your depression *in order to avoid thinking about yourself.*

Moving on up the ladder, we can allot some monthly depressions for younger women and some chronic depressions for older women to the chemical basket—although again, not *all* of them and *not automatically.* If you have reason to suspect that a hormonal factor is the villain, before you toss it carelessly into the chemical basket, look to see if there are any concomitant factors. By and large, hormonally induced chemical depressions are hand-in-hand (or arm-in-arm) factors—you almost never find them walking around all by themselves. So in acknowledging the chemical portion of your depression, don't be satisfied to say, "I'm menopausal, and that's that"—especially if you're a man. Look for the companion or companions to your hormonal blues. Hormones are seldom, if ever, the sole cause of a bad downer. The "divide and conquer" idea is the best way to approach this one—handle each component separately. For example, if you're depressed because you're menopausal, you are also probably down because you're worried about aging. And on top of that, you may have health concerns. Handle each concern in its own right. What people do to combat depression about aging is a multi-billion-dollar industry, so obviously there's plenty you can do about *that;* and the health and physical-fitness businesses are flourishing too; if you have the time and money, you can make a career out of your looks and your physical condition.

Chemical depression can be brought on by alcohol or drugs which you have willfully introduced into your body. Talk about idiocy—how about overimbibing alcohol because you are depressed! Using alcohol or drugs (chemicals) to mask depression is the most common form of self-treatment—and, ironically, it is a most destructive and inadequate way of dealing with the very problems you are attempting to assuage. It's destructive because alcohol and drugs *increase* your depression, and it's inadequate because they camouflage the causes of your unhappiness. When you use chemicals to avoid thinking, you end up sloshing around in them and in your problems forever.

Finally, the most serious forms of chemical depressions (I use the plural here because there is more than one form and more than one cause) can have to do with malfunctioning glands, inherited and troublesome endocrine systems, serious nutritional deficiencies, disturbances in the interfunctioning of the body's systems which might disrupt normal chemical balances, or the body's inability to utilize chemicals normally. As you can see, this end of the chemical depression scale is very complicated and calls for some very sophisticated handling.

The field of chemotherapy in the treatment of depression is still in its infancy—the use of lithium carbonate in treating manic-depressives didn't get off the ground until the 1960s. (Actually, this new field is called "pharmacotherapy" and involves highly individualized treatment programs which are tailor-made to the patient's personal set of conditions, mental and physical.) There are now whole different families of drugs that can have benefits for the person whose depression is caused to some extent by chemical problems. It's important to do some careful screening if you suspect that there is *even a possibility* that your problem could be chemical. In fact, after you get through checking yourself out with your regular M.D. to make sure that you haven't got any common disease bugs and that your diet is giving you good nutrition, you might look into getting some fancy checkups to see how your body chemistry scores. I will offer one or two other ideas for what to do about chemical depression in chapter three, when I talk about how to handle your depressions once you have recognized them for what they are.

Barometric depression, the other half of chemical, is even more obscure than its mate. Nevertheless, you can recognize that there are forces at work *outside of you*—such as ions in the air or phases of the moon (one of the possible arm-in-arm links to hormonal depression), or a pending storm which can tip the balance toward feeling down when you are on the borderline. Barometric pressures are usually quite subtle in their effects, and I prefer to think of them as inducive of melancholy rather than depression—except, as I have said, when they hit you in combination with other problems, or when an individual is uncommonly sensitive to their presence. (Barometric influences can also cause you to go absolutely berserk when the moon is full. Moon-bayers will attest to this, but that comes under the heading of "crazed," "moonstruck," or "in love"—not depressed.)

While you are thinking about yourself in relation to chemical or barometric factors, keep in mind that you are a very complex creature. Many different elements are constantly interacting within your body. You're full of chemistry and electricity—and so is the outside world. Among the myriad internal and external factors that are operating and interacting at any given moment, so much is happening to affect your mood that it's a wonder you manage to stay on an even keel so much of the time.

Entertainment depression is the third type. I'm not even sure that it should be called a type at all, since it could easily be discussed as an aspect of barometric or habitual depression.

In my opinion, entertainment depression is the most interesting of the down conditions, and the most creative. Possibly it is the type of depression we least like to own up to, for in giving value judgments to depressions, entertainment is considered the most reprehensible.

What do I mean by entertainment depression?

Picture a dark, rainy day (here's where the connection to barometric comes in). You're home, propped up in bed reading poetry. Perhaps Verlaine's *"Il pleure dans mon coeur/Comme il pleut sur la ville . . ."** Oh how sweet, how ineffably sweet to taste the sad, poignant feelings that overtake your sensitive soul. (If you haven't read Verlaine, you might like to.) And if the radio in the background is playing "Walse Triste" or a song of lost love, so much the better.

There's nothing in the world wrong with enjoying the flavor of melancholy once in a while, *if*—I'd like to be able to print that word two inches high right here on the page so you'll be sure to get the emphasis—*if you really do let*

---

* "It weeps in my heart as it rains on the city . . ."

yourself enjoy it! For a sensualist such as myself, melancholy can be a beautiful and extremely pleasurable emotion —especially when you consider how many genuinely sad things there are in life that need to be contemplated now and then. I, for one, am not too crazy about people who are always so busy or so deliberately distracted that they shut out any awareness of those delicate passing moments. I certainly don't have time for the artificially hearty and robust types who never let such an "unhealthy" or "decadent" emotion flood their beings.

Melancholy, in my view, is not a negative or sick emotion. Melancholy, as an exquisite shade of sadness, as a fine tonic of gentle sorrow, is in high repute among poets and romantic lovers. Or at least it used to be in high repute, and I'm interested in restoring its former stature.

I qualified the word *lovers* with the word *romantic* for obvious reasons. The sensation of sadness associated with love-making (those who *only* have sex won't know what I'm talking about) has long been recognized by writers. And now the psychologists are getting into it—in connection with orgasm, which is also referred to in French as *le petit mort*. Certainly it is easy to view the moment after orgasm as a time of "pleasurable melancholy." In sum, entertainment depression has a legitimate time and place when the full-hearted enjoyment of it is *not* reprehensible. So don't let anybody talk you out of it.

Like all good things, however, it can be abused. Depression as entertainment is not good when it is used as a means of overcoming boredom. Again, here's where you have to think about yourself before you think about your problem. Squint your eyes and take a hard look. Then ask yourself this question: "Was I feeling bored before the blues hit me?" If so, there's a very good chance that you were subliminally aware of the pleasurable side of entertainment depression, and you pulled it out in order to create a little fun and excitement. Feeling down is better than feeling nothing.

The only thing I have against this is that there are so many *other ways* to achieve the same results without the side effects—activities you can enjoy directly while saving your melancholy for its own positive enjoyment.

You will notice that I always opt for the direct over the

indirect. It's more economical. Besides, you have to be very careful about how you use entertainment depression, because it can be habit forming. (See habitual depression.)

Sparingly experienced, entertainment depression can contribute lovely dark hues to your emotional palate, and it can enrich and deepen your brighter, lighter emotional tones. Overdone, it loses its positive side and eventually the pleasurable sensation of melancholy is dissipated and lost to you altogether.

Any downer which does not get sorted out and put into one of the other three baskets will end up in the habitual bin.

Habitual depression is the type that can do the most damage. This kind is closely related to a point of view or a response which makes you *set yourself up for bad news*. People who suffer from habitual downers are often so cynical that they see the bleak side no matter what happens to them. They are always on guard against disappointment. They guard so much that hardly any joy can ever get through. This reminds me of the story about a certain cigarette which was supposed to steady your nerves. A wag I know remarked, "Yeah—I smoked those cigarettes. They steadied my nerves so much I couldn't move!"

It's possible to be so steeled for the blow that your habitual *stance* becomes a *cringe*. Who wouldn't be in a perpetual depression about how rotten the world is and how nasty it treats you, if they saw everything from a cringe?

You have to be especially careful to guard against habitual depression setting in when you have suffered from a long run of bad luck and the resulting circumstantial depression. Rigorous self-analysis is necessary to keep you from succumbing to the temptation to expect the worst, when day in and day out you've been getting it in the neck. The motto "Be Prepared" does *not* mean cringe every time somebody raises a hand to wave at you. If it did, can you imagine the posture Boy Scouts would end up with? A raised hand may have given you a slap in the chops any number of times—and may again and again. But raised hands also deliver a friendly wave or a pat on the back.

Don't duck before you spot what's really coming at you. Each and every time is different. I don't care how many times you've struck out before—each and every time you come up to bat is a new time!

What I am talking about, of course, is the "fate" issue. You are *not* predestined to fail time number 1,000 just because you didn't succeed the first 999 times. I know this because I once read a book on the law of probability (actually, the book was on the odds of winning at gambling, but odds are based on the law of probability). The law of probability is based on the long run. There's one small hitch. The long run can last more than one lifetime. Eventually, odds do even out—but we all know cases when the "evening out in the long run" didn't do much for the individual who was hanging around and waiting. He or she couldn't last that long. This fact of life can be depressing as hell if we let it. Some day I'd like to make a list of all the poor writers, composers, painters, and so on who went under saying, "I'll be recognized in the long run." I won't think about it right now, however, because that would depress me.

By recognizing the long run as a fact of life and by playing the odds, you can figure that although the long run can run right off the board, *the odds are in your favor that the turnaround will come in time to do you some good!* Also, keep in mind that the same law of probability that gives you a seemingly endless run of bad breaks can give you a seemingly unbroken run of good breaks. I'm sure you've witnessed both aspects of this law in your time. And you've got just as good a chance to get it on the good run as on the bad—better, if you've been on a bad run for a long time already. *Just don't give up in despair and quit in the middle of a run.*

It must be mentioned that you can affect the odds. Your attitude and expectations can influence how things fall out for you. I'm not willing to go whole hog and say that *all* prophecies are self-fulfilling, or that you are responsible for *everything* that goes wrong (or right) in your life. I believe there is such a thing as luck. I have seen it—bad and good—and I have heard luck cursed and blessed by others who believe it exists. I believe you have to make your effort to achieve success . . . and then hope to get lucky. Being optimistic only helps you to act in your own best interests. So, be optimistic. It can't hurt.

When I was talking about how to determine if your depression is circumstantial, I mentioned three questions dealing with self-blame that you might ask yourself. Self-blamers (SBs) never allow *anything* to be circumstantial, chemical, barometric or entertainment! SBs belong, lock, stock, and barrel, with the habitual bunch, because they always have to take the blame for everything: Nothing can be anybody else's fault; nothing can be due to circumstances beyond their control. In fact, SBs steadfastly refuse to acknowledge that there *is* anything such as outside circumstances or luck. By automatically blaming themselves, SBs don't have to face up to or deal with their real problems. If you suspect that you are sometimes, often, or always an SB, I urge you to get yourself a victim basket and concede that it is *possible* for you to be a victim occasionally. If you get yourself the basket, perhaps I can persuade you to use it.

To recapitulate: there are four basic types of depression. They are distinct but interrelated. Before you can take action, you have to figure out which one is your dominant type of the moment. In order to figure that out, *you have to think about yourself*. Then you can think about what to do to get out of your depression.

Most people do not know how to think about themselves. They think about what's bothering them and think that that's "thinking about themselves." The difference between those two is about the size of outer space. The best story I know to illustrate what I mean is the one about the old southern cook who always cried when she peeled onions. After years of seeing Georgia cry during this chore, the woman she worked for noticed that Georgia was *not* crying during a particularly long onion peeling session. When she commented on this, Georgia answered with a smile, "Them onions done got used to me." This was Georgia's way of thinking about her problem—she simply projected it onto the onions! Thinking about what's bothering you has got to come *after* you've thought about yourself. By that time, you'll be able to look at your problem in a constructive way. It so happens that this is precisely the thing that most shrinks try to get you to do. They word it their own way, of course.

Most of us are uncomfortable thinking about ourselves. There's something slightly embarrassing about it, as though it were a sign of extreme vanity to be interested in looking at how you think and feel—the way it's slightly embarrassing to gaze too long or too often at the way you look in a mirror or a snapshot. My opinion is that you should be interested in how you look, think, and feel! These are part of your vital signs. Taking an interest in yourself is an indication of a healthy ego, and in my book, that's not only a good idea, it's a necessity.

You. You are unique and special—which you've already heard so often it's like "Close Cover Before Striking." Who pays attention? But there it is—you are! Consider: Only you know most of the slop that went into making you the miserable wretch you sometimes feel yourself to be. And only you know about all those dreams and hopes and visions of how you wanted it to be.

If you've gone to a shrink, you know it can take years and God knows how many thousands of dollars for you to train one to know you. And even then, being human, it's possible for the shrink to get things mixed up and need you to put him or her back on the right track.

I'm suggesting that it's both cheaper and quicker for you to pitch in and do a lot more of the figuring out by yourself. Believe it or not, this is exactly what your shrink wants you to do. Everybody will be very happy about it.

Forget about being objective . . . nobody is, or ever was —not even two dozen shrinks acting as a committee. In fact, especially not two dozen shrinks acting as a committee. Nothing that has to filter through the eye, ear, nose, or throat of a human being in order to get to the brain can be objective! However, we can try for a little distance occasionally, in order to get some kind of perspective on ourselves. (Myopia gives you a poor perspective for dealing with depression—microscopes can be helpful sometimes, but myopia, never.)

How do you achieve a little distance?

Suppose you have had an encounter with someone that left you feeling depressed. It might have been your spouse, your boss, your lover, your friend. It might have been your mother, your father, your sister, or your brother. It might have been a total stranger. The point is—afterward you felt depressed and you didn't know exactly why.

Try casting yourself, and the other person(s) in the piece with you, in a repeat of the action. Use the words, gestures, body language of the actual scene (as much as you can recall) but put yourself outside the action for the re-run. You're observing this time. Now see if you can catch your own act, your own role, in order to see what triggered your depression.

This is what I mean:

Let's say that you have invited one of your friends over for dinner. Your friend calls and says, "Would you mind very much if we make it another time? My cousin Beth is in town for the weekend and wants to see me . . . I've got a ton of work to do before Monday . . . and Liz is in a dither because she doesn't know what to do about getting ready for the painters. I promised her I'd come over and bail her out."

Accommodatingly as usual, you answer. "Yes . . . okay, I understand. We'll make it next week." And you hang up.

Pow! You feel rotten and down. Why?

This is an easy one (but then, other people's are always easy).

As you go over it, you recognize that you felt angry but *you didn't express what you were really feeling.* You avoided the confrontation. You hid your hurt. You agreed to your own rejection. By "understanding," you were an accomplice in your own put-down. Not only were you angry with your friend, you were angry with yourself for your own complicity!

Unexpressed anger or hurt frequently is the trigger for depression.

In replaying the scene, you can clearly see what happened and why. Your friend put two other people's feelings before yours; you didn't even come in second. It is not necessarily because the other two are preferred to you. But because *you allow yourself to be put last,* you set yourself up for a habitual depression.

Now you can take affirmative action. You can call your friend back (better late than never) and say, "Look I'm really angry and I'm giving you notice that I will not tolerate that kind of treatment again."

Respect is born. You respect yourself and your friend respects you. Your self-esteem is salvaged—enhanced, in fact, because you feel proud for having the courage to say what you felt and for having risked disapproval. (Incidentally, your friend's reaction may include surprise and irritation before the respect shows up. You'll have to weather that.)

Next time you are in a situation with this kind of potential, you can try to express what you're feeling on the spot. *The sooner the better.*

When you consider how many negative self-images are contained in the example I gave, is it any wonder that the you in this scenario felt depressed?

Catching on to what triggers you is a very valuable piece of information to have about yourself. Seeing what you do to set yourself up for a downer is equally important. Catching on to what triggers the other person isn't bad either, especially when you're in an intimate relationship with someone and things don't always go terribly smoothly.

A second way to achieve a little distance is to put yourself in the other fellow's shoes, in order "to see yourself as others see you"—which is about the right distance in this instance.

Now let's look at it again:

You and your friend have known each other for a long time. Your friend needs to be needed and wanted. You have never objected to being reshuffled before; in fact, your frequent and easy acquiescence to canceled dates has conveyed the feeling that you are not especially keen to see your friend anyway, so what harm is there in breaking a date with you *in order to be with people who do care?*

From that little distance, you can not only understand your friend better, you can also learn something more about yourself. Remember, thinking about yourself requires hawk eyes that don't blink, which makes you resemble a cross between a bird and a snake. But who cares about looks at a time like this?

You have thought about yourself. Good! But remember

that every time you're in the pits, you have to think about yourself vis-à-vis this *particular* pit.

There are always multiple aspects to our depressions. The causes, as well as the effects, overlap. So we must become sophisticated about analyzing which causes are primary, which secondary, which tertiary, and which plenipotentiary. I have broken them down into basic types merely for convenience so that you can look at them separately for once. But I don't need to remind you that in real life, a depression hits you like a lead ball right in the middle of your chest. After you've been zapped, catch your breath and then begin to take the lead ball apart by analyzing its components. Once you break it up (or down), you've got a shot at dealing with the parts one by one.

Dealing with things one by one—one piece at a time—is a first-rate coping device. *No matter how many things you do, take them one at a time.*

CHAPTER 2

How to Tell When You
(or Someone Else) Are Depressed

"Opposites" is one of the fundamental characteristics of depression. Shrinks talk about manic-depressive behavior, for instance, and it seems clear that you may be as depressed when you are feeling up as when you are feeling down. The opposite is only the other side of the coin.

Let's say that something is bothering you but you haven't figured out what it is. You may alternate between opposite kinds of behavior such as silence/chatter, fleeing from/dwelling on, being giddy/being glum. Any number of opposites may come into play.

Alternating between them can be a form of disguise—one of the tricks you play on yourself as a means of hiding from, obfuscating, and otherwise confusing and beclouding what you are really depressed about. Like a kind of alternating current, this device is a substitute for the direct expression of what you are feeling: the direct current. Depression thrives on the feelings you do not express directly. Anger, frustration, resentment, even love and tenderness that you have not permitted yourself to experience as what they are, can be experienced as depression. You must learn to switch away from your indirect, alternating current—from AC to DC, as it were. You make the switch by first figuring out what's really bothering you—this is why everything starts with learning how to think about yourself.

To help you remove some of the disguises in which depression cleverly hides, let's consider some of the corresponding guises.

Opposites

One of the signs of depression that isn't always recognized as such is the "silent" symptom. A whole lot of silence emanating from somebody doesn't always signify profound thoughts. More often it means a fierce depression which has taken the form of silence because there is such a crowd of mean feelings choked up inside that the exit has gotten mobbed and nothing can come out. Picture a revolving door on the first of the month at your bank, jammed with everybody trying to push out at the same time. Result: nobody can get out—everything is all choked up. Conversely, if the mob manages to break down the doors, instead of silence you get the opposite—endless prattle, everything rushing out at once. What appears to be contradictory behavior may not necessarily be two different things. Depression finds (or makes) its own exits. Front door or back door—active or passive—may very well be the same mean mob coming out in two different ways.

Two other well-known opposites which are manifestations of depression are "dwelling on" and "fleeing from." When they take the form of paralysis and incessant motion, these are the passive and active parallels to silence and endless chatter. The person who is constantly on the go is just as likely to be exhibiting a classic sign of depression as the person who cannot move.

I think it is possible to employ your symptoms themselves as a means of helping counteract the effects of your depression. If science has learned to use half-dead bugs to build up a resistance to highly virile ones, why can't you use some of your bugs to overcome the discomfort they produce?

44

You might, for example, elect to do some conscious fleeing in order to give yourself some temporary relief or gain some time. By consciously choosing to flee, you use the symptom rather than remaining at its mercy. Recognizing what you are doing and acknowledging why you are doing it is tantamount to killing the bugs before you inoculate yourself with them.

Try to identify your own patterns of depressive behavior and then you can begin to use them to combat your blues. Do you smother/withhold, for instance? Or cling/abandon? Once you recognize which form your depression takes, you can use its opposite as an antidote. For example, if you feel that your grown child doesn't call you often enough or pay enough attention to you, perhaps your offspring feels you are "clinging" and is reacting to you by what you feel is "abandonment." In this case, *you* stop calling (in effect, you do the abandoning) and see how fast your offspring will also reverse behavior and start calling you. Or if your husband/wife accuses you of "smothering" and reacts by "withholding" his/her own demonstrations, turn the tables! Withhold your affection and see how fast your spouse comes looking for it. Not only will you counteract your inner feelings of depression which are attending whichever of these traits you possess, but the chances are good that by reversing your outward behavior, you'll also achieve responses from those around you which will make you feel still better. If you're a dweller, try some fleeing for a change. If you chatter, try being silent. Naturally, it is always easier to see the patterns in others before you learn to see them in yourself. But we all have them, and the important thing is to face them rather than run away.

Speaking of running away, "fleeing" (I use this term to describe all types of behavior for avoiding facing problems) is the most common symptom of depression. The reason it is the most common is that you use the things that give you the most pleasure and enjoyment in life as a means of escaping from facing your problems. This is why it is so difficult to spot the depression behind fleeing: you are doing things that are "good" for you, things that are relaxing and fun—and it never occurs to you that they are serving as an escape mechanism.

Inner Demons

Prime time for a lot of intense fleeing is between three and four o'clock in the morning, when your inner demons come out for their constitutional. (If you keep them pushed down out of sight and out of mind all day and most of the night, they'll sneak out and demand attention when your guard is down.)

Since your inner demons are what you're running away from most of the time, I'd like to discuss ways of dealing with them besides frantic escape.

First, you have to make their acquaintance. This means letting them out *when you choose*. It means talking to them. Confronting them. Airing their grievances. In short, it means developing a relationship with them—which you cannot do as long as you are running like mad in the opposite direction!

Stop running.

Turn around and look them square in the eye (located in the center of your forehead).

Find out what their demands are.

Then, enter negotiations.

All of the above should be done on a regular basis, like meetings between labor and management—because you *are* labor and management. You must not wait until they go out on strike at three o'clock in the morning and *force* you to give in or run for dear life. An ongoing parley serves the best interests of both parties.

When you face your inner demons without hysteria, you'll be surprised at how reasonable their demands are. I've never understood why some people get so upset when demands are made on them. After all, demands are only your psyche's shopping list, and *everybody has needs*.

You may also be surprised at how well your inner demons behave when they know you care. Giving them a chance to gripe and demand is an excellent way of demonstrating that you care. It also relieves the pressure. Like any intimate relationship, you'll have your ups and downs

—but being friends is a lot better than being mortal enemies. Remember, you're in it together.

These suggestions for taking your inner demons (your ID) out for regular walks are a preventive nostrum—a sort of "flee prevention" prescription. But it takes time and skill, which must be developed through application and practice. What do you do in the meanwhile, before they stop snapping at your heels? Once you have begun to know them, you can use some fleeing by design in a constructive, healthful manner. In chapter seven, I offer you a whole list of Modes of Fleeing, which includes many of the "good" things you enjoy doing. Use them consciously when you need temporary respite, and your enjoyment should double with the knowledge that you're in control.

Depression is a funny thing. We all go around using expressions like, "I'm depressed," or "It's depressing," to cover a hundred different feelings that we haven't bothered to sort out. We may be miserable, unhappy, disappointed, disillusioned, bitter, desperate, despairing, disconsolate, downhearted, grieving, downtrodden, exploited, distraught, frustrated, dispirited, fed up, or simply tired. But we slap the label "depressed" on whatever "it" is somewhere under the *Ds*. It's interesting to note that so many bad states of feeling start with the letter *D*—but that's no excuse for filing them all away under the word depression and letting it go at that. Starting right now, eliminate the word *depressed* from your self-descriptive vocabulary. When you want to describe how you feel to yourself or others, think about it precisely; what *exactly* do you feel? What word or words describe your mood most accurately? Then use the correct word or phrase. *You cannot deal with your downers until they are clear in your own mind.* (You will permit me to continue to use the catch-all terms, I hope, because I am talking about the *general* condition, whereas, you will be talking to yourself about your *specific conditions.*)

Depression is also funny because it is often colorless, odorless, and tasteless. In other words, you may not be able to see, smell, or taste anything. You may not admit to yourself that you're suffering (the workaholic thinks he's ambitious, not depressed) because you aren't letting yourself feel anything—even though on some level you know it's there. The shrinks have a lovely phrase for this absence of feeling: lack of affect. I like it because it rhymes. The only drawback is that it's *serious*. Apathy may be a very effective way to deal with pain. But I think it's a bit expensive—like using a bulldozer to snuff out a cigarette butt.

Feeling pain is not something I enjoy, but shutting off all feelings in order to prevent pain is throwing the baby out with the bathwater. Psychic pain, like physical pain, has a function. It indicates that something needs attention and care. When something hurts, it is telling you to look after it. Therefore, you should think of pain as a signal—a call to action. The only way to get real relief is to give the hurt area care and treatment, and then allow time for healing.

And then there's all that *good* stuff out there to feel too, so not feeling anything as a means of blocking pain is not my idea of a smart tradeoff.

However, not feeling anything at all is an extreme, and there are many degrees of numbness which come before rigor mortis sets in. This is one of the reasons it is so important to recognize your depressions and get to know them.

You need to attack the big *D* and break it up into bite-size pieces. Then deal directly with each piece.

Depression can take many forms, and your attempts to outrun it can also take many forms. When you run away, except by design, you always know somewhere inside you that the big *D* is still there waiting to catch up with you. This can make you feel more depressed than ever, causing you to try to flee still harder.

The two-step approach will enable you to deal with it on the immediate-relief level and on a deeper level.

Recognize your depressions for what they are.

Choose your nostrums and use them by design.

For those of you who do not live alone, I advise you to take your cohabitors into your confidence and tell them about the nostrums you will be choosing to use and why.

They have a lot to gain by giving you support and encouragement, because depression is a highly contagious condition—and when you feel better, so will everyone else you live with.

Your spouse's reactions can be particularly important to your success in coping with depression. Your spouse should realize that although it can start out that way, depression is not simply a "bad mood." *Mutual* understanding is necessary. With it, your nostrums will be far more effective and your motivation for sticking to them will be much greater.

PART II

Relating to and Coping with Your Depressions

CHAPTER 3

What to Pull out of the
Bag of Nostrums, When . . .

Let's say that you have now looked at yourself and decided that this time your depression is, indeed, circumstantial. The likelihood, incidentally, is very high that it will be circumstantial, since most of the time, with the less serious depressions, you can pinpoint the event that gave you the sendoff. (Aside from the frequency of the circumstantial factors in causing depressions, I am placing it first because, as I mentioned in Chapter One, everybody is subject to this one at some time in life, and if it is dealt with quickly and adequately, it can be prevented from developing into the more serious kind of habitual depression.) The nice thing about circumstantial depression is that you can immediately haul out your resources, muster the troops, and gird your loins for action. Your very first piece of action is *broadcasting*.

Broadcasting

Pick up the telephone and call one or more of your *real* friends. One of the reasons I advise you to do this is that you're going to do it anyway, so I may as well prove how wise I am by suggesting it right off. When asked how he

53

got along with Margaret so well, President Truman answered, "First I find out what she wants to do and then I advise her to do it." I include *broadcasting* under action because, though you may not think of it as such, you are already beginning to help yourself when you tell your troubles to a friend. The act of talking is the initial step toward getting relief. When the guano clogs up the air conditioner or the shit hits the fan (I offer you a choice because somebody objected to the use of the first phrase on the grounds that it was too slangy and vulgar—or maybe it was the second. Anyway, you may have circumstances that require both phrases.), as it does in a circumstantial depression, *you're entitled to some sympathetic understanding from your true friends*—so by all means, gather it in. It won't make you feel sorry for yourself, but will reinforce your conviction that your downer is circumstantial and you've had a rotten break. This sets you up for being brave and courageous and resilient in the face of adversity. And believe you me, you may as well believe that you are all those things, because you'll need to be.

Did you notice that I qualified the word *friend* with the word *real* and the word *true* in the last paragraph? These are important qualifications, because getting the right response is very important at this stage. Let me offer a few criteria for determining real and true friends:

1. A real friend knows you well enough to realize when you need to be listened to.
2. A true friend cares enough to listen truly even when his/her own preoccupations might dictate doing something else.
3. A real and true friend responds to you by saying positive things generously and negative things constructively.

Keep in mind, however, that even within the realm of real and true friends—if you are lucky enough to have a realm—you must exercise discretion. I will give you some guidelines on which real and true friend to select under which circumstances in chapter seventeen. Selecting *who* to tell *what* to is crucial. This is because you are always looking for a certain kind of reaction and not other kinds of reactions, so you can't afford to make a random selection.

After you call your friend or friends (just remember I caution you to be sure they're real or true—because this is not the time to find out if they're otherwise), if you still need some more air time, you can fill in your supply of ears by calling people who have recently been through similar circumstances themselves. Co-workers who also got the same ax, for example. They'll be very understanding and may even have a good idea or two to exchange with you. Finally (but only if you run short of the previous choices) you can call the people who call you every time disaster strikes them. Only use these types in an emergency, because they're fraught with a lot of dangers—such as being so full of their own problems that they can't be bothered with yours.

At this point, you've made contact with humanity; you've broadcast your woes sufficiently to feel satisfied with the injustice of it all. Now you're ready to begin doing something more constructive.

Step two is to acknowledge that the entire world is stocked with victims like yourself, and that at some time or another, everybody takes a turn at it. This translates to, "I needn't feel paranoid, it's just my turn." From there, you can work around to, "If everybody else can handle it, so can I!" This may seem obvious to you, but you must still *say* these things to yourself. You need to hear them and that's *not* the same thing as knowing them in your head. I think it was Freud who commented that when you say something out loud you should be careful because your subconscious is listening and hears what you say—or words to that effect.

This leads you to step three, which is comparison.

Comparison

Comparison is a marvelous bolsterer—especially when it's made of down.

Here's how you do it. Remind yourself about a friend, Mary D., for example. "Do you remember how well she handled it when her husband ran off with a nurse two months after Mary finished putting him through medical school? If Mary D. could handle *that*"—you say to yourself—"I can handle *this!*"

Or:

"How about stalwart Philip C. who had to stand by helplessly and watch firemen break through his living room wall (destroying the heirloom tapestry worth at least $25,000 that had been in his family for two hundred years) in order to save the eighteen-year-old dog of the family who lived next door when, in a drunken stupor, the lady of the house lit the sofa instead of her cigarette.

"Philip was a model of fortitude. If he was—I can be too!"

By comparing my troubles with theirs, and by reminding myself how impressed I was with *their* good grace and stability, I arrive at the conclusion that I can handle *my* disaster with equanimity. After all, I'm made of just as sturdy stuff as they are! What's more, I've waded through worse patches than this in my time!

Broadcasting and *comparison* are necessary as a kind of foundation. They serve to shore up your ego and self-confidence. Ego and self-confidence are the best two legs in the world to stand on when you're trying to pick yourself up off the floor. In addition, broadcasting and comparison serve another function: they give you a little *time* to recover your balance after the blow. Because circumstantial depression usually catches you off guard, the blow tends to send you reeling. Don't try to force yourself to take dramatic action the instant after you've been struck. You need a bit of a breather to let your brains have a chance to stop spinning. The techniques I have outlined will prepare you for the dramatic steps that you will devise as part of your campaign to find a new job; get your tapestry rewoven; or make your ex-husband repay the money you put out to educate him (thereby enabling you to go to law school at night). Practical planning requires a clear, confident head. Once you have regained your composure, you will be able to tackle the practical actions with ease. The minute you start planning and executing your plans of action, circumstantial depression disappears!

56

In chemical or barometric depression, the "doing something about" is rather straightforward. If it's chemical, and on the less serious end of the scale, you can stop whatever you're doing to foul up your natural healthy mix; you can get a medical checkup to see if there's a physical cause to your imbalance; you can adjust your diet if there is some nutritional deficiency; or you can take something (under medical supervision, of course) to supply whatever may be missing from your system.

I would like to point out that when I speak of chemical depression, I am talking about the everyday, normal kind of imbalance—the kind that fluctuates periodically during the day or the month and returns to normal limits by itself (or with a little help). It should be noted, however, that there is a whole school of thought that emphasizes chemical causes as the basis for *all* depressions. The proponents of chemical treatment for depression make their own case. As I said earlier, extreme and/or totally debilitating depression are beyond my purview and I am not competent to judge or comment on the efficacy of chemotherapy—or pharmacotherapy or ECT—for depression. I know of at least two books on the subject of pharmacotherapy, both written by leading exponents of drug therapy, for depression. They are: *Moodswing* by Ronald R. Fieve and *From Sad to Glad* by Nathan S. Klein. These volumes make interesting reading for anyone who wants to explore the subject of pharmacotherapy as a treatment for depression.

In the words of Dr. Michel R. Mandel, director of the somatic therapy unit at the Massachusetts General Hospital, ". . . drugs prove effective in about 65 to 70 percent of the most severe depressive illnesses. But that leaves a large 30 percent of these patients who are just not having any response." Dr. Mandel has found a much higher success rate in the treatment of the very serious cases of depression by the use of ECT (electroconvulsive therapy) —90 to 95 percent, in fact.

There are pros and cons for both pharmacotherapy and electroconvulsive therapy. If you want to find out more about either, do some asking around and begin reading some books, pro and con. There is a recent report put out by a task force of the American Psychiatric Association on ECT. And there are also books by critics of ECT. For the extreme end of the depression scale, careful study and consideration should be given before making any decision as to which kind of therapy to begin.

In general, waiting will solve many of the downers I characterize as chemical or barometric. In chemical depression, your internal mix is changing constantly and will right itself sooner or later, unless the depression is caused by a chronic condition that needs medical attention. The same thing applies to barometric—except that it is the *external* balance that has gone temporarily haywire and will right itself if you wait. (If you don't want to wait, you can go to a steambath, take a sauna, or get on an airplane to someplace else.)

The main thing about chemical or barometric depression is to *recognize* it at the time. That seems simple enough, but it isn't always so easy in practice. If you even suspect the vague possibility that your problem could be chemical, it's more than worthwhile to go to your doctor for a medical checkup. A doctor will be able to spot the cause of your problem even if you don't, and you'll find it easier to weather a chemical or barometric depression once you've realized what it is—after all, that's where the expression "weathering it" probably came from! Just remind yourself that your cloud of blues is in the process of lifting this very minute. Now is the time when distraction is a good chaser. I'll be offering you some suggestions for short-term measures beginning in chapter six.

The next type of depression is the one I have named entertainment, and we could do with some about now. Frankly, this is my favorite—there's nothing like an occasional good brood to enrich the personality and flavor the soul. I realize that not everyone enjoys this sort of thing, so if you don't savor melancholy, just read this section to see what to guard against. As I indicated earlier, the crucial thing about brooding is to be out front about it— open and honest with yourself about what you are doing and why. You're entitled to brood once in a while if you feel like it. I said brood—not sulk, seethe, whine, or grieve. Sulking is for infantiles. Seething is for detonation (just before you blow up). Whining is for nags. Grieving is for mourners, who are expressing one of the most profound and important emotions a human being can experience. Don't demean grief by using it as an entertainment device. I am referring to people who bemoan, mourn, or grieve over unpleasant events in a manner which partakes of the tragic, whether or not the cause is large or small.

Entertainment depression generally occurs because you're bored. There's too little stimulation coming your way. A big fat depression will get your juices going, if only negatively—and *some* feeling is better than *no* feeling. Obviously, the cure for entertainment depression (if it's melancholy it isn't depression, so just lie back and enjoy it after you make the distinction) is to find things to stimulate you that make you feel good, not down. Or, if you've got to feel a soupçon of down, then try compassion for someone else—that will give you the darker emotional tone you may legitimately need or want at the moment, and it's infinitely better for you than your depression.

Stimulation

You have noticed that I repeatedly advocate drawing delicate and precise distinctions between your different states of feeling and the various responses to those feelings. As human beings, we are capable of a tremendous range of emotions. This capability is one you should use not only in dealing with your depressions, but in the normal living of the richest possible life. The more emotional variety you have, the better. Variety is absolutely vital to human beings, because one of our basic needs is for stimulation. Right along with food, sleep, and water goes stimulation! You've got a head full of brains that demand material to chew on and sensual experiences to connect, relate, and make coherent to thoughts. I say, feed 'em! I say explore as many new paths and avenues as you can, both within yourself and outside yourself.

Explorers are never bored. Adventurers are never at a loss for things to keep them interested and interesting. And if you're busy exploring and having adventures, you won't have time or need for moping.

Where stimulation is concerned, the ticket is to find things to care about. Put out for things and people; get involved in somebody else's struggle; have a stake in what happens to other people's dreams or projects. You can even get interested in how the repaving of the sidewalk is progressing down the block. *Anything and everything* that interests you can be stimulating. I have seen how stimulating other people's struggles and trials can be, as I watched a number of my good friends alternate between sheer frustration and tremulous hope while empathizing with me. They shared my feelings of rejection or encouragement, and they shared my hopes for success (thought not, admittedly to the same degree that I did). These precious friends became involved with me; and in so doing, they now share whatever happiness I find and pride I take in having waded through the miasma. These friends have made an emotional investment in me and in my dream, *and I have in theirs*. In no way do I, or do they, diminish any personal goals by investing in someone else's.

Investment, therefore, is perhaps the best answer to boredom and lack of stimulation. When you make an investment—emotional, financial, physical—you take a certain risk. The element of risk is what adds spice to the game, and spice is stimulating. The more you have at stake, the more excitement you will feel while you await the outcome.

Investing is active and positive—rather than sterile, like depression. The nice part about investment is that you can invest all over the place at the same time: in yourself, in others, in ideas, in causes, in bingo games—as well as in tennis matches, in elections, in the outcome of the world series, in the seeds you planted in your flower pots, in budding dance companies, in research programs for disease, in the state lottery, in volunteer service, in the Olympics, and on and on and on. The more things that hold interest for you, the better. The more you invest, the more interests you will develop and the more you will *have* to invest. Investment increases exponentially and works for you, because when you are invested in more than one race at a time, you can hedge your bets. There is always something you can hope to win on. I say invest not only in more than one race at a time, but in more than one horse in a given race. Invest . . . invest . . . invest . . . your time, your energy, your money, your hopes, your talents, your love, your ideas, your whatever. Everybody has something to invest, and if you spread your investments around, you'll soon discover that you're so busy keeping track of all your various investments that you don't have time to be depressed by your fair share of losses or failures. Failures and losses are natural. When you've invested solidly and wisely, there are always ways you can still win.

Once in a while, a long shot will pay off, and once in a while, a sure thing will lose. Invest enough and it will all even out in the long run. Meanwhile, the odds are good that you'll stay on an even keel because multiple investments are an insurance policy against the dangers of single-basket egg-putting.

Now we come to habitual depression. Of all the ways to be depressed, and of all the causes, this is the hardest to overcome. It is the most elusive, the most diverse, the most prevalent, and the most stubborn. It is ten times harder to beat habitual depression than it is to give up smoking or drinking or even overeating—and interestingly enough, it is related to those three bad habits. I intend to devote all of chapter sixteen to an in-depth discussion of that relationship. But for the moment, let me just make a few general observations. In breaking any habit, there are certain comforting gratifications you are required to surrender. Habitual depression, like any other habit, is a two-pronged hook: First, you are hooked on the unthinking familiarity of being in the same old rut—you automatically respond to a difficult situation or problem by getting depressed; and second, you're hooked on the satisfactions you get from being depressed—which is what you are doing instead of taking action. An old heartache can be very comforting and also stimulating when there's nothing *new* to think about. These are potent satisfactions, but they're not invincible.

Let me go on record by saying that *I believe in soothing*. I even soothe myself by calling myself endearing names such as honey or baby or even darling once in a while. I believe in soothing so much that sometimes I wrap my arms around me and pat myself when it's necessary and there's no one else around whom I want to do my soothing for me. *But not habitually!* In other words, if soothing is appropriate, then by all means *soothe*—go whole hog, soothe yourself whole-hoggedly. But habitual depression as a means of soothing yourself is too indirect—it's strictly second-rate soothing. You aren't clear about exactly what you are doing or why, so the soothing is underhanded and watered down. (And it isn't easy to be both at the same time).

One of the worst aspects of habitual depression is that it is basically a dishonest response. On top of being dishonest, it's careless and lazy. When you receive painful stimuli or have unpleasant experiences, there are many, many legitimate responses you might have. So if you simply respond with an automatic habitual depression, you aren't truly experiencing whatever happened to you, and therefore you will not be able to deal with it.

Habitual depressions are defenses. (Have you ever noticed that the hardest thing to take about people is their defenses?) This type of response creeps up on you when you've had a long run of bad luck or a series of failures. You begin by feeling that you've been wrong so many times in a row that the only way to be sure you are right is to join in with your opposition. So you put yourself down and predict the coming blow before it arrives. Then you say, "I knew it!" and be right about something for a change. The trouble with being right in this way is that it's a sure-fire downer—and if you notice the words *put yourself down*, you'll realize that it's *deliberate*. You've done it to yourself! Trying to prepare for a blow is human and understandable, and for those of us who ride too high and fall too hard, anticipating the least can be a form of self-protection. (I said anticipating the *least*, not the *worst*.) The longer habitual depression goes on, the more dangerous it is. The danger is that being in a habitual depression can become a way of life.

As a practice questionnaire for getting used to thinking about yourself, look over the following list and place yourself where you think you belong. Remember that habitual depressions don't come in black and white. They come in degrees and shades. On the following scale of one to ten, rate the color of your response when things don't go the way you want them to. Then judge for yourself how much of your problem stems from the responses you make to unfavorable circumstances. Judge for yourself at which point you think your circumstantial depression turns into a habitual one.

When things don't go the way I want them to:

My Response Is:	I Say Things Like:	Color My Depression:
1. to take it as the natural course of events	"That's the way the cookie crumbles." or "That's par for the course."	lavender
2. wryly self-deprecatory	"I did it again!" or "I need a keeper!"	morning-sky blue
3. automatic cynicism	"What else could I have expected?" or "If it *hadn't* soured I'd be surprised."	evening-sky blue
4. self-blaming	"If there's any way for me to louse myself up, I'll find it." or "I can't do anything right!"	cobalt
5. self-pitying	"Why do I always have such rotten luck?"	gray blue

My Response Is:	I Say Things Like:	Color My Depression:
6. bitter and futile	"What's the use?" or "Nothing good can ever come of anything for me."	ashen
7. vindictive	"If I can't have anything that I want, I'm certainly not going to be nice to anyone else!"	indigo
8. ultimatum issuing	"If things don't improve soon . . ."	midnight blue
9. desperation	"I don't know how much more I can take." or "I'm at the end of my rope!"	charcoal grey
10. the pits	"The only thing left for me to do is kill myself"	pitch black

If you catch yourself using any of those phrases as a standard answer when something does not work out as you wished, watch out! You're probably on your way down the line of habitual depression. As you can see, this type of depression tends to get progressively worse.

I think it is worth repeating that you set yourself up for habitual depressions. Once you see how you do it to yourself, you can develop ways to interrupt the pattern and find a blocking device which deflects the usual flow of your responses. Use the same technique to break the habit of depression that you would use to break any other habit.

Depending on *you,* determine whether you should try to cut down a little at a time or whether you have to go cold turkey. The temptation will be there for you as it is in the other addictions. Resisting or controlling it will be just as hard. The best hope I can offer is that once you become aware that this.kind of depression *is* a habit, you have a somewhat better chance than you had before. Chapter 16 will offer suggestions for acceptable alternatives to help you break the habitual-depression habit and feel better while you're doing it.

Rejection

Now I want to go into the feeling that goes with losing. It is probably the single largest element in depression—you can feel it in almost any situation in which you have invested and lost.

In mentioning Mary D.'s case and how her husband left her for the nurse, I touched on rejection as a source of depression. This is a biggie. Before you can take action when rejection is involved, you've got a lot of thinking to do. If it's an emotional rejection, you can't afford to just stand there and say, "I got rejected because I'm a piece of garbage," or "I'm not worth being loved." Oh no you don't! Not only is that a cop-out, it's a cheap shot, because feeling sorry for yourself relieves you of having to figure out what went wrong. Lazy . . . very lazy. And you are bound to repeat whatever went wrong again and again, unless you figure it out!

Begin with a fundamental question:

What did John want that I didn't offer?   -

Now scrutinize John's needs, wants and expectations with exquisite care, without putting yourself in the picture. When you have thought about John and what he wanted as thoroughly and completely as you can, *then* peer intently at yourself.

Ask these subsidiary questions:

Did I realize before I offered myself to John that he wanted something different?

If I *did* realize it, why did I offer myself anyway?
Am I willing to change myself to be what John wants?

When you have answered the subsidiary questions, you will find yourself with some very useful insights about your behavior patterns. You may be able to think about yourself in a new way. This leads to a second fundamental question:

What did I offer that John didn't want?

Now you must scrutinize *your* needs, wants, and expectations in terms of your desire to be accepted.
Ask these subsidiary questions:

Would it be more suitable to change whom I'm offering myself to?
Should I have looked for someone who wanted what I was offering in the first place?
Could John and I both give a little in terms of what we are wanting and offering each other?

When rejection occurs, supply and demand have not matched up someplace. Either what was supplied was not demanded, or what was demanded was not supplied. (I am using the word *demand* in the sense of "ask," of course.)

All these questions require a great deal of thinking, but by thinking ahead, you can eliminate a helluva lot of painful rejection in the future. The answers will allow you to see whether a particular rejection was due to circumstances (mistakes happen), in which case you deal with it as a circumstantial depression and get over it in good time, or whether you set yourself up for it, in which case you've got yourself a habitual, and it's time to start breaking the pattern.

The rejection issue isn't confined to love affairs or even human relations. The genius who coined the phrase "rejection slip" for writers must have been a cross between Jung and Shakespeare. Let me assure you that getting your rejection in the form of a slip from a publisher or a telephone call from your agent is every bit as painful as a verbal rejection from your lover, spouse, or friend. Being turned down hurts, whether it's your offer of love or your labor of love. It's how you deal with the pain—what you do with it—that counts. You may learn that you want to change, that by gaining the insights into yourself through looking at what happened you have already begun to change. If, on the other hand, you reach the conclusion that what you offered was pretty special, you may have to face the fact that you've offered it to the wrong bird (you've sent your masterpiece, the result of your life's study on herpetology, to a publisher of true romances). The results may be interesting, but they won't lead to acceptance. The principle is the same when you've offered your sensitive soul and gotten rejected because the object of your affection is looking for business contacts in bed. You may get leafed through out of curiosity, but you're bound to end up rejected. I, for one, don't want to waste my time getting leafed through—not my book, nor my body.

Know thyself and thy offerings and size up *whom* you offer them to in terms of whether or not there is a decent chance for a matchup between supply and demand. (I didn't say *perfect* matchup, I said *decent*.) I'll go along with sanding off a few corners and rounding the edges to fit a square into a round hole any time. Don't use too much force, but some frictional adjustments won't hurt you or the round hole.

Beware of one fly which sometimes gets into the ointment: are you *looking for rejection?* If you stumble on that one during your self-examination you may benefit from some professional help in arriving at the bottom of *why*. But if you can rule out the possibility that you're into rejection as a means of self-flagellation for nefarious misdeeds and disgusting bad habits which have persisted since childhood (such as bed-wetting, nail-biting, or killing off one or more parents in your head), you can line up your target—the recipient of your offer—and feel confident that your firepower will be more effective the next time around. It's surprising what aiming will do!

Intention

Another word for aiming is *intention*. In the process of analyzing what was wanted that you didn't supply and what you supplied that wasn't wanted, you came upon the intention factor. All artists and creative types become intimately acquainted with intention—and since human relations are the grist for the artist's mill (particularly the writer's), I am constantly trying to apply everything I know about the creative process to human relations (and vice versa). You might say that I try to grind all my grain in the same machinery.

Once you get the flour from grinding your grain, you can make bread or cake or spaghetti. The basic ingredient —understanding or insight—is what is "kneaded." Intention comes in after you have ground the grain. "What am I going to make this time?" you ask yourself. "What is my intention?"

You have to decide whether it's going to be strudel or sourdough bread or pretzels before you can proceed with the subsequent steps. If you're feeling practical, you may look around and decide on the basis of what the demand is for and make *that*—unless you are absolutely dying for strudel and you are mainly interested in satisfying your own demands. But whichever the case, you must be clear about your intention before you start baking.

How does this translate into your relationship with John?

Let's go back to the basic ingredient again. Let's say that after examining John's needs, you discover (through your basic ingredient of understanding) that he wants croissants and nothing *but* croissants from you. You decide to whip up a batch to make him happy. But maybe you've never made croissants before and they come out tasting like strudel. Or maybe they come out fine, but then you *alternate* between making croissants and strudel. Either way, *your intention was to please John and you failed*. Now you have a wonderful opportunity! If your intention to please John holds firm, you can find out what went wrong in the baking process, correct it, practice a lot, and end up making the best croissants ever. You will have to give up the idea of strudel, however. By figuring out where you missed, you can correct your problem. You can do something. As soon as you see what you have to do to please John—presto, your depression will vanish because you will no longer be rejected. *John will want what you offer.*

On the other hand, if you perceive that you can only offer a compromise, at best (croissants alternating with strudel), then your intention is to meet John halfway. If he can't meet you halfway, you must withdraw your offer *without feeling rejected* since you have fulfilled your intention and John's demands become his problem. *Not your lack!* You have control over your intention and that gives you control over what happens to you. As soon as you have some control over being accepted or rejected, you will find that your depression instantly evaporates.

It's amazing, but true: the minute your head gets to work on what misfired and caused the rejection, you'll be so busy figuring out whether you want to change your offer —and if so, how—that you'll be home free.

The last possibility is that you will remain as adamant in your offer of strudel as John is in his desire for croissants. When this happens, forget John and look for another recipient. Try another lover, or try another publisher or try a dozen—but do a little research first, if only to save wear and tear and postage. Find out as much as you can (before you submit your precious offering) about the tastes, needs, predilections, values, style, and flexibility of those to whom you would make your offering. Of course, if you've got no patience for research and you also have a very tough hide, you can do like the sailor who said he always asks thirty women to go to bed with him the minute he hits port—at least one of them will say yes. Nothing wrong with the scattershot approach if you've got the hide of an elephant. Keep your devil-may-care attitude —not everybody cares about quality.

Knowing your intention is an important piece of information that comes out of thinking about yourself. You have to take all your quirks, foibles, and warts into consideration. It may be somewhat disquieting at first, but don't be discouraged. You'll find that thinking about yourself (which leads to thinking about others) is rewarding in many ways. When I think about myself, I have to admit that I'm difficult. This means that those who appreciate me tend to do so in bits and pieces, and the rare soul who can take a big chunk of my whole package only comes along now and then. As Katisha remarks in *The Mikado,* "It takes me years to train someone to love me."

Knowing that I am this kind of person, and accepting my intention to express the real me, I must then accept the fact that it may indeed take me years to train people to love me. I also know that I am many-faceted and capable of presenting the lighter, easier sides of myself when it suits me. Not everyone can love you and not everyone can accept the whole you. Rejection has its place in the natural order of things, and it must always be regarded in relation to your intention.

Only you can decide how much rejection you can tolerate over the long-distance run from someone who is important to you. In the beginning of most relationships, there is high hope of eventually being *totally* accepted by your spouse, lover, or friend. This very rarely happens. But if you aim for understanding, you'll find that acceptance is easier—on both sides.

Someone I know says she allows three major shortcomings in any one friend, and after that she has trouble accepting more. My own feeling is that you can accept people with their flaws when they're worth it to you. If the relationship doesn't offer sufficient compensations, you tend not to accept very much.

The most important thing, of course, is accepting yourself. There are things you can change and things you can't change. If you can tell which is which, you're a long way toward gaining your own and your companion's acceptance. Ongoing rejection of some part of the essential you either will cause chronic chafing or eventually you'll seek acceptance elsewhere.

One of the chief rewards of coming to know and accept yourself is that you develop patience—especially with yourself. Your goal should be to become the world champion self-knower and self-accepter. As Gerard Manley Hopkins (our brother in depression) wrote me in one of what are called his "terrible" sonnets, "My own heart let me more have pity on."

I repeat that line to myself quite often—in fact, whenever I find myself coming down too hard on me. Some of the components that make up your depressions *are* serving you as punishment. You have to keep your eyeballs peeled for the ways in which you beat up on yourself. You know and I know that there is enough punishment out there already. So when you catch yourself laying it on—knock it off!

By way of illustration, I like to tell the story of what once happened when I was a small tyke of about ten or twelve. I locked myself up in the bathroom with a thousand-page novel and one of my father's cigars. An hour or so later, my mother saw me emerge, my face the shade of early spring. She took a look at me and watched me retreat to my bed to lie down, but she never said a word of remonstrance. Years later, I mentioned the incident to her, asking if she had known what I was up to. She had known, she told me (the reek of my father's cigar was unmistakable), and she had correctly assessed that I was already having all the punishment I needed without her having to add to it.

In general, those of us who go in for self-punishment are usually getting enough of it already. If you've got the guilts about whatever, throw them out and get tough with yourself: either you stop doing whatever it is you feel guilty about, or you stop feeling guilty about whatever it is you're doing! To feel guilt *while* you're doing something creates a standoff—you spoil whatever fun you might have had and you open yourself up for some heavy downers because even if you stop, you still want to do whatever it was. A friend of mine—who is a very smart lady and happens to be a terrific A-number-one shrink—said she would like to abolish three things from the face of the earth: war, poverty, and guilt. Think about it. And think about the company that guilt is keeping in that context.

So you have thought about yourself. You have thought about what kind of depression you're in. If you were rejected, you have thought about why you were rejected. You have examined your intentions and decided whether you carried them out. You have either recognized the desire to change what you're offering or decided to offer it elsewhere. This has taken a lot of thinking and a lot of sorting out. Good! Depression is not a huge, amorphous lump, as many people think. It is truly a variety of discrete states. And you must get in the habit of thinking about your depressions with discrete labels.

I want to emphasize that the nostrums I recommend are not designed simply as distractions. The very opposite is true. I am suggesting that you confront your enemy—grab hold of the horns and wrestle like the Furies. I am suggesting that you work at curing the *causes* of your various depressions, and that you begin to do this by knowing your enemy. Recognition is a big step, and the moment you begin to use your brains to work on something positive and constructive, the blues begin to fade.

Action is the best cure for depression.

Thinking is the strongest action.

CHAPTER 4

Ploys and Plots for Jockeying Yourself out of It

Take a piece of paper and write the following on the left-hand side of the page, leaving ample room between each line:

The circumstances: _____

The immutable facts: _____

My resources: _____

Possible sources of help: _____

Additional circumstances: _____

Coordination of efforts: _____

Creative gain: _____

Now imagine that the circumstance at the core of your circumstantial depression (a health problem, the breakup of your marriage, a job loss, financial woes) is a huge boulder sitting smack dab in the middle of your potato patch. The time has come when you can no longer plow around it—it's in the way and you've got to do something about it!

Write in the real circumstances which are causing your depression and, as we talk about the boulder, translate the steps I suggest so that they will suit your situation. Try to fill in each of the subsequent items on the list as we go along.

Budging Your Boulder

Don't just pick up the first branch you can find and start prying away—all you'll succeed in doing is wearing yourself out and destroying the branch. Random prying is strictly no good. If you manage to budge it an inch, you'll be lucky.

What you have to do is step back and look at it. Look at it hard. Walk around it. Circle it in your head and regard it from every angle while you consider it.

Looking at boulders and considering them is an art. It shows respect for your problem—and believe me, a problem *that* size deserves to be shown respect. This is the stage at which you are taking in the immutable facts from all different angles (if it's a health problem, you may be waiting to see if it gets better by itself or responds to home remedies; if it's a job loss, you may be taking a few days off to re-do your résumé or consider some training to gain new skills). You're beginning to figure out how you can budge it, and you are doing this *before* you lift a finger to touch it.

Next you think about *your resources* in dealing with this particular boulder (will it help if you stop smoking, go on a diet, ease up on your work load; should you study at home or enroll in night school?). "How heavy is it?" you're asking yourself. "Can I lift it in my two hands? Can I push it with my foot? Where can I get an iron bar for leverage?" you ask yourself when you begin to think about possible sources of outside help. "Will Farmer Brown next door help me? Can I borrow his mule? How about dynamite?"

These are some of the questions you might be putting to yourself as you walk around considering your boulder from all angles. You are moving nicely down the list in figuring out a way to budge it.

After due consideration, you may decide which approach is best to try *first*. There's no guarantee that you'll be able to move it on the initial attempt, but all that thinking and considering before you make the first attempt will cut down on your exertion and save you a great deal of frustration. If you fail on the first try *after* considering, then you will learn something from the failure which will hone the considerations that lead to your second try. Accept the fact that budging your boulder is bound to take more than one effort, and that each effort is not a failure but a learning process which is guiding you closer to your eventual solution. For example, if your problem is learning to live as a single after your marriage has broken up, you may try a singles group, find it not to your liking, and be ready to join a different group of kindred spirits united by a common cause or interest *other* than meeting singles. You've refined your effort by learning that not just any group will do. Now you're ready to be still more selective, and your second shot should come much closer to the target.

Like a game that requires planning, plotting, and ploying, you have to keep a lot of factors in mind at the same time. Chess players and bridge players do this all the time. If you catch on to how it works, you'll be able to improve your moves in everything you do. The real trick is to *make the moves in your head first,* as a way of testing them out. Like taking your show on the road before you open on Broadway, this try-out enables you to make changes and rewrites before you are committed to a costly production. (The wear and tear and friction you save yourself would have been very costly indeed.)

Try-outs in your head do not guarantee that you'll never make a mistake or miscalculation. Nor do they insure against overlooking a potentially *better* move—especially when you're new at the game. But the more you play it, the more expert you become, which will give you its own special kind of gratification, not to mention how adept you will become at boulder-budging. (So, as well as looking for the best groups to join, you will also be considering whether you are still too shy to take advantage of the group setting at this time, or whether the lack of spontaneity, with all those other singles trying to make new contacts, is disturbing to you.)

In addition to saving you wear and tear, mental try-outs can be used in a number of other ways, which we shall be delving into at appropriate places. The technique of using the mental or imagined experience offers you all the advantages of the physical "real life" run-through and eliminates the drawbacks. The key to mastering this valuable technique is to use your imagination to create a *real* experience totally within your mind. Just as you experience real feelings when you dream, you can also experience and learn things from what you live through in your imagination.

When you are selecting your ploys and plots, keep in mind that the most up-to-date treatment for a number of knotty problems is a barrage—the combination of this and that seems to produce better results sometimes than just this or just that. You might, for example, try pushing your boulder while the mule is pulling—or get someone else to work the leverage while the mule is pulling and you are pushing. (The person who has lost his or her job will be registering with agencies *while* sending out letters and résumés to personnel managers *and* answering classified ads *and* making inquiries through friends about openings they may hear about.)

Try several different approaches together and separately, in different combinations or in various sequences. Devise unconventional or innovative moves and carry them out *in your head*. Even if you do not end up using any of them, freeing your mind to range as far and wide as it wishes— without fear of making a mistake—will lead you to new possibilities. One of the chief problems associated with circumstantial depression is the fear of making a mistake and compounding the problem. Fear inhibits you from conceiving the many alternatives open to you in seeking solutions.

Following through with the boulder, you have reached the stage where it is wise to consider what will happen as a result of any steps you might take. This is the "additional circumstances" item. (If you borrow money, would it be better to put up your insurance policy for collateral at the bank or take out a second mortgage? Should you sell the family heirlooms or your stocks?)

You must think it through. For instance, if you use the dynamite, it will certainly blow the boulder to pieces, but the blast may also knock down the outhouse—not to mention scaring the eggs out of the chickens. Here's where you might begin to make some adjustments to come up with a finely tuned barrage. But first review what you have achieved and learned so far:

1. You've toured your boulder and ascertained a number of facts.
2. You know it's too heavy for you to lift with your two hands.
3. It's too deeply embedded to push with your foot or move with the leverage of an iron bar all by yourself.
4. Farmer Brown may help you and may lend you his mule.
5. Dynamite is a last resort.

Next, you probably should walk over and have a talk with Farmer Brown. (This is the point when you might get a second opinion from a specialist, seek counseling, take aptitude testing, or talk to your accountant.)

Farmer Brown says that his mule is not only stubborn, but lazy. He suggests that you ask Farmer Green if you can borrow his tractor. Farmer Brown volunteers to lend you his chain and grappling hooks—he's dealt with boulders of his own—and he offers to help you attach them. You thank him for sharing his experiences and giving you good advice and help, and you telephone Farmer Green right then and there so you can arrange a mutually convenient time, if Farmer Green agrees to let you use his tractor. (This is like being referred to an employment agency that handles the special kind of job you're looking for—they've got the best equipment for what you need.) You set the date for next Monday. As soon as you hang up, Farmer Brown says to you, "Where do you intend to put the boulder?"

You haven't thought of this at all and you're stymied. Since the boulder is in the middle of your potato patch, it's a long haul to drag it clear of the entire planting area. Farmer Brown, being experienced in potato patches also, understands the problem (which is why he raised the question) and makes another valuable suggestion: "Why not move it away from the outhouse and the hen house *first* and then put a small charge under it—just enough to break it up so you can cart off the pieces?"

You now have a viable plan—at least to begin with. So you go off to secure the dynamite.

Your first stop is to talk to Neighbor White, who is always going around blowing up things and is the local expert on backyard demolition. He recommends the quantity he thinks you need to do the job and tells you how to place it. He even decides to sell you some of his, since you can't get any delivered in time for next Monday.

When Farmers Brown and Green arrive, you are ready. You attach the chains, pull the boulder a few hundred feet until it's far enough away from the hen house and the outhouse. You set the charge and you all retreat to await the blast.

It works!

Not only are you boulder-free, but you have decided to use the rocks and rubble to pave your driveway—so you're ahead of the game. You've even made a creative gain.

The outhouse is intact, and the chickens found the whole experience rather exhilarating.

In the process, Farmer Brown and Farmer Green got better acquainted and had a good time. You have made yourself available to them for any help you can offer in the future and you've learned something from each of them. The next time you have a boulder to budge, you'll be able to attack it with more dispatch and more confidence.

The story of the boulder demonstrates the fact that dealing with any circumstantial problem or obstacle requires a lot of fits and starts: much gathering of information, advice from those who are in the know, planning and coordination of effort, analyzing and adjusting of approach to adapt to unanticipated ramifications, and so on.

Remember, however, that you did a lot of figuring out by yourself before you asked anyone for help or advice. When they gave it, you considered what was said very carefully—and if it made sense, you followed it gratefully.

As a practice device, think of three or four circumstantial depressions you've suffered from in the past. Choose different kinds: job loss, health problem, loss of spouse, financial troubles . . . whatever. Now take another piece of paper and fill in each circumstance:

	Job Loss	Health Problem	Loss of Spouse	Financial
The Circumstances:				
The Immutable Facts:				
My Resources:				
Possible Sources of Help:				
Additional Circumstances:				
Coordination of Efforts:				
Creative Gain:				

Fill in each line item by item as best you can for each of the different circumstances. Be as complete as possible as to what you did *then*. If there were things you left undone, leave them blank. Then go back and try to think of steps you MIGHT have taken then but didn't. Finally, fill in things you might have done to help yourself under each of the different conditions that caused your circumstantial depression. This will aid you in learning HOW to apply this technique to current problems. It will give you practice in the all-important habit of figuring things out and being creative.

Figuring Things Out and Being Creative

Figuring things out is a time-honored occupation. It is also a unique, characteristic, and noble activity of the human mind. What puzzles me is why, if we love to figure things out, we have such a resistance to figuring out *ourselves*. We're pleased to figure out what makes the other person tick, but before shrinks, it was practically a disgrace to figure anything out about yourself.

As far back as A.D. 270, the Roman philosopher Plotinus wrote: "Feelings can be present without awareness of them," and "the absence of a conscious perception is no proof of the absence of mental activity . . ."

Throughout history, first philosophers and then psychologists have been discussing and arguing about conscious *versus* unconscious mental activity. In 1690, the Earl of Shaftesbury wrote: "One would think, there was nothing easier for us, than to know our own minds . . . But our thoughts have generally such an obscure implicit language, that is it the hardest thing in the world to make them speak out distinctly."

Aside from the difficulty we have with thinking and with understanding the process of thought itself, I believe we have only recently (relatively) started to become really self-aware. And the experience of self-awareness can be overwhelming. painful, even alien.

I think there may be a number of reasons self-awareness or "conscious perception" or making our thoughts "speak distinctly" has always been so difficult. Until we were freed from having to be on the lookout for danger practically every minute of the day and night, our minds were quite preoccupied with exterior events. We were turned outward and used our brains primarily to handle outer situations. Self-awareness arrives along with certain kinds of luxury. When everything out there is calm and under control, we have the luxury to consider areas that never got much attention before. Societies where life is unspeakably hard—because of climate, or lack of food, or constant warfare—don't produce art. They don't allow for introspection or self-awareness, because survival is taking up everyone's energy and attention. And, as I've been saying all along, this thinking, cogitating, considering, and self-study is essentially a creative process.

Also there is a certain amount of resistance to being self-aware, because most of us are somewhat afraid of what evil things may be lurking in our subterranean caverns just waiting to spring. We are afraid of unleashing demons. We are afraid of being overwhelmed.

Erich Neumann writes, ". . . the conscious state is the late and uncommon phenomenon, and its complete attainment is far more a rarity than modern man so flatteringly pretends, while the unconscious state is the original, basic, psychic situation that is everywhere the rule." Elsewhere he states, ". . . the unconscious is not in itself destructive and is not experienced as such by the whole, but only by the ego. Only during the early stages does it feel threatened . . . later, when the personality feels itself allied not only to the ego but to the whole, consciousness no longer sees itself threatened to the degree that the adolescent ego was, and the unconscious now presents other aspects than those of danger and destruction. What the ego experiences as destructiveness is firstly the overwhelming energy-charge of the unconscious itself, and secondly the feebleness, liability to fatigue, and inertia of its own conscious nature . . . we shall always find that fear of the unconscious, and fear in general, is a symptom of centroversion, seeking to protect the ego. . . . The tendency of unconscious contents (of the mind) to swamp consciousness corresponds to the danger of being 'possessed'; it is one of the great 'perils of the soul' even today."

In a similar vein, C. G. Jung wrote, ". . . the devaluation of the psyche and other resistances to psychological enlightenment are based in large measure on fear—on panic fear of the discoveries that might be made in the realm of the unconscious. . . . It is this fear of the unconscious psyche which not only impedes self-knowledge but is the gravest obstacle to a wider understanding and knowledge of psychology. Often the fear is so great that one dares not admit it even to oneself." *

Cervantes said, "Make it thy business to know thyself,

* *The Undiscovered Self.* (A Mentor Book, published by The New American Library.)

which is the most difficult lesson in the world." And Lincoln Barnett said, "Man is thus his own greatest mystery. He does not understand the vast veiled universe into which he has been cast for the reason that he does not understand himself . . . Least of all does he understand his noblest and most mysterious faculty: the ability to transcend himself and perceive himself in the act of perception." A Tibetan monk, Kunto Zangpo, blamed the endless stream of human suffering on the failure of most individuals to perceive their source in universal mind. "May all beings," he prayed, "recognize their own radiant awareness."

The opposite of being overwhelmed by our unconscious mental powers is to underestimate them—to take them too much for granted. We take many ideas about the world for granted—ideas developed by human beings, not provided by nature. Figuring things out is a gift each of us has naturally. We must learn to tap into the part of our mind that creativity comes from—the unconscious—and use it by bringing it to consciousness. Each of us has the seed or potential for creative thinking. We can use this potential not only to enrich our lives but to help us solve the problems of living.

So many of the great contributions to civilization which we no longer think about (we take them for granted) are the result of somebody's creative problem-solving. Euclidian geometry didn't just grow like trees and bushes. Once upon a time there was this guy named Euclid walking around like you and me with his own boulders to worry about. When *he* decided to budge *his,* he walked around them plenty. Talk about considering all the angles. Look what he came up with! Boulder-budging hasn't been the same since. Which shows you that sometimes what you figure out about budging your boulder may help someone else (or even mankind) with theirs.

Today there is an enormous interest in studying how the brain works. There are biologists, psychiatrists, psychologists, physicists, chemists *et al* engaging in experiments all over the world. The lines of demarcation between disciplines are disappearing as discoveries in mind/body relationships compel scientists to criss-cross areas. Even the language being used to describe findings in biophysics has begun to sound like what we once might have thought of as metaphysics or poetry. Fascinating and accessible books have been written on the subject: Maya Pines' *The Brain Changers, Scientists and the New Mind Control* (Harcourt, Brace, Jovanovich); *The Brain Revolution* by Marilyn Ferguson (Taplinger); *Explorers of the Brain* by Leonard A. Stevens (Knopf), to name just a few. The findings described in these books are mind-boggling in their implications: At the University of California at Berkeley, for instance, a team of scientists (David Krech and Mark R. Rosenzweig, psychologists; Edward L. Bennett, biochemist, and Marian C. Diamond, anatomist) found evidence the *the brain actually changes with experience.* They discovered that when rats are given challenging toys to play with or problems to solve, their brains actually become heavier!

Experiments being conducted by Dr. Elmer Green at The Menninger Foundation's Psychophysiology Lab are aimed at training people how to go into states of "creative reverie." Dr. Green also believes that if there is such a thing as psychosomatic illness, there is also psychosomatic health: the same forces are at work in both. He is engaged in studying how "will" enters the picture in physical health. His research combines bio-feedback techniques with autogenic training. (Autogenic training is a system of self-regulation developed by Dr. Johannes Schulz early in this century. It combines some of the self-control aspects of yoga with some techniques taken from medical hypnosis.)

Dr. Robert Sinsheimer, of the California Institute of Technology, believes that through genetics our brains will continue to develop and improve as they have been doing since the beginning of time. Compared to future generations, we will be viewed as having very small brains, "Frail and slow in logic, weak in memory and pale in abstraction, but . . . on occasion possessed of innate common sense and uncommon perception" . . . small genetic changes might "expand our consciousness into unknown sensations and into undreamt intensities."

From many diverse voices representing diverse interests in man's potential come positive, even fantastic predictions about our future development. Loren Eiseley has

83

suggested that man may be slowly achieving powers over "a dimension capable of presenting him with a wisdom he has barely begun to discern."

You do not have to wait for a vague "future" or pass up the advantages that these scientists are saying will belong to those who follow us. *Your* brain has a tremendous unused potential. You can use *your* brain in ways that you have not taken advantage of before. Your brain is there, waiting to be put to work to help you figure things out. In fact, it's working on your problems even when you are not aware of it. Begin to tap its powers and they will serve you in many, many ways. Start by feeding the facts of the matter you're trying to figure out into your brain (which is what is happening as you walk around considering your boulder); do a little cogitating on some of the tangential issues (such as the proximity of the out- and chicken-houses); fill in whatever information you need (how much dynamite to put where); and then trust your brain to do the rest. Not only will it organize the entire proceedings for you, but it will contribute added creative touches of its own (such as making a gravel driveway out of the debris).

When you do not give your brain constructive work to do in figuring things out to help you, it will find *other* things to work on. This is one of the chief instigators of depression. Have you ever noticed that people who don't have big boulders to worry about will aggravate themselves to death over little ones? Your brain needs to puzzle and solve and work on solutions. You crave the moment when that light bulb goes on inside your head and you holler, "Eureka, that's the answer!" The "eureka experience" (which is really the creative experience) is one of the most exciting and thrilling things in life.

The ability to discover is not limited to mythical beings who exist in some kind of rarefied atmosphere and who have strange names like Euclid or Bach or Rembrandt or Einstein. One *you* start to enjoy thinking about and considering and figuring things out, you will be using your creative faculties as surely as any artist or scientific genius who ever lived. *The process is the same.* Whether or not it leads to an earth-shaking contribution remains to be seen, but one thing is certain—you will come up with a whole new way of looking at your problems. Using your mind creatively is the best defense against *not* using it destructively.

Remember this: your brain is the strongest muscle in your body! If you can think about it as a muscle, you will be more likely to think about using it in a new way—you don't have to be hog-tied by conventional ways of thinking about anything!

It is well known that many athletes do much of their practicing in their heads. They go through the actual play, work on improving form, overcoming problems and strengthening weak points *all in their heads*. Time and time again it has been proven that they can improve their game this way.

Nor is this mental workout restricted to athletes. Vladimir Horowitz, the great concert pianist, does almost all his practicing in his head. Artur Schnabel, another great pianist, hated practicing so much that he spent very little time at the actual keyboard. Most of his preparation for an actual performance was done in his head. By the time he got his hands on the piano, they were already well-rehearsed in the piece. You have to admire and respect anyone who can fit a concert grand into his head, not to mention getting in there with it and practicing. (Junior, however, may not be quite ready to give up his exercises, since this is an advanced technique.)

But you can learn to do it too. You can use it to improve your golf game or your tennis or your bowling; you can use it to improve your bridge game or your chess game; you can use it to rehearse job interviews, court appearances; or public speech making—you can use it for anything that will improve by being rehearsed and practiced. Remember, this is something you do all by yourself —you need no audience or listeners. Everything you need for your practice or rehearsal is already in your mind. Problem solving is a mental process. Thinking is a sport played in the mind. Develop your brain muscle and train yourself to use it.

You can learn, imaginatively, to fit the entire universe into your head—so there shouldn't be any trouble fitting in a boulder or two. Being creative isn't a sacred gift reserved for a chosen few. Working in your head isn't a faculty reserved for mental giants. We all can do both.

CHAPTER 5

How to Turn Anger and Self-Disgust to Your Advantage
or
When You've Bitten Off More Than You Can Chew Don't Sing the Blues with Your Mouth Full

What you hear most often about habitual depression is that it is repressed anger. What you feel most often about habitual depression is self-disgust. These two are partners in crime, because when you repress your anger, it turns inward and takes the form of self-disgust.

You got angry in the first place because of some frustration—the blanket may have been wrapped around you, confining your little arms or legs too much; or the bottle of milk did not arrive when you wanted it. And you got *mad!* Red in the face, screaming, bawling mad. This was entirely proper behavior, but it didn't make Mommy and Daddy very happy. They didn't encourage it.

So when you got a bit older, you began to get scoldings (or worse), and you started controlling these displays—or at least modifying them. To a degree, you had to learn to control and modify . . . to a degree. But some part of you learned too well and controlled too much and ended up unable to express anger at the right person at the right time for the right reason. Unable to release it, you swallowed it—and by now, when we zoom in on you, it's sticking in your craw in great, indigestible globs. You are lying there with a bellyful of self-disgust. You despise everything about yourself—everything you are, everything you aren't, everything you ever have been or never will be, everything you never tried to do and everything you ever did. *Despise* (one of the *D* words) is passive; that's why you're *lying* there—despite is self-disgust at its peak.

It is possible to release your anger, instead of repressing it, and put it to work for you by turning it outward. Anger is active. It will get you up to *do* something. And, as you know, doing is the best cure for depression.

The reason anger is included in our quiver in the first place is that it is a very potent, concentrated form of energy—when we need a fast, forceful shot, an arrow of anger can go right to the mark.

If you observe fighters and other sports participants, you will see how they use anger—it comes in several different forms—to give themselves an extra charge. Because it is concentrated energy, anger can be called on when an emergency presents itself and that added charge is needed, or when the body is deenergized for some reason and instinctively signals for an infusion by making you feel irritable. You then get the missing energy and are able to take action.

Depression is a state of deenergization. Therefore, when you call on anger, you are actually calling on a source of power to spur you to action. The action in this case is anything you do which is of benefit to you.

When you *release* your anger as a source of motivating power, you must also *direct* it toward a situation which is related to some source of frustration in your life. You must devise your tactics, mobilize the troops, and deploy them toward the taking of a predetermined objective. Anger then becomes a drive—a goal-oriented drive. You will find that many people have used just such a form of energy to boost themselves to the top. Anger can, in this way, be a component of courage and success—when it is used properly.

But several words of caution are in order.

Your anger must be directed toward the real source of your frustration or the real cause of your difficulty or the real nature of your problem. All too often we turn anger toward the wrong target—either an innocent but handy bystander (usually a loved one), or ourselves.

Be sure to steer your anger only toward what you are *not doing*.

Leave who and what you are alone. Give it a rest. If you are doing things you don't like, leave that alone for the moment too. These problems will ease up by themselves when you begin to use your anger constructively.

If you find, however, that you have a hard time leaving your self-disgust alone—and that because of it you have trouble using your anger—then I suggest that you can link your self-disgust and your anger to *humor* and turn them to your advantage.

In one sense, humor is a form of rebellion against the critical faculty—the "judge" within each of us who issues ultimatums about what we should or should not do. We know that our inner judge is very sensitive and hates disapproval from outside. In order to insure that we don't get negative feedback, the judge inhibits us from expressing "unpleasant" emotions like anger.

Joking enables you to circumvent your judge's rulings on things which, if you did or said them seriously, would be deemed unworthy. In other words, humor can be used as a way of getting around, guarding against, or otherwise quieting your own self-criticism—the "judge." You can use humor to express truths or acknowledge problems that you might have trouble expressing in an undisguised way.

Freud said that "jokes are envelopes for thoughts of the greatest substance." The saying, "Many a truth is said in jest," attests to the fact that by masking your intent with humor, you can get away with voicing it. Freud also said, "Anyone who has allowed the truth to slip out in an unguarded moment is in fact *glad to be free of the pretense*." (Italics are mine.) "In jokes," says Freud, "nonsense often replaces ridicule and criticisms in the thoughts lying behind the joke."

Jokes are a system of release and, as such, can be used to combat depression just as anger can. But putting an important but difficult-to-handle thought about yourself or someone else in the form of a joke, you make it more palatable. You slip it by the judge by making it give enjoyment first—and the meaning follows in a secondary manner.

We all like to laugh. When we're feeling in good spirits, we laugh more easily. When we're not feeling in good spirits, laughter can help cheer us up or ease the tension. That's why we instinctively tell people a joke when we want to help them feel better. We can also use laughter in the form of humorous self-deprecation to bring ourselves up from crying to poking fun at ourselves.

A friend of mine who is an executive in an advertising agency told me that she has been miserable and depressed lately about her job, because her clients (she handles three or four major accounts) are all constantly criticizing. Nothing pleases them. Nothing is enough to suit them. This constant griping has so worn her and her boss down that he has taken to sticking his head in her office door just before the end of each day and asking, "Is anything all right?" The wry humor they share is the only release that makes the incessant criticism bearable. Together they can laugh at the problem—and by laughing, they reduce its importance.

Recently I heard a comedian on TV deliver the quintessential joke for the habitual-depressive type: "Things are looking up," he said jovially, "bigger and better things are falling through."

Woody Allen's "depressive" humor is his trademark. Almost all his offhand observations replace thoughts that would be intolerably depressing if they were expressed directly, with poking fun. His fun-poking is, a wry admission of the real causes of his depression. He not only succeeds in relieving his own pain, but we all laugh with him at jokes in which we see ourselves. Self-deprecation is at the root of his humor. He is the psychological sophisticate who has been through years of therapy, knows all of his own hangups and games, is semidetached and therefore able to watch himself going through his own routines. Allen's depressed condition, interestingly, does not affect his ability to work. He is successful both in real life and in his films. He has learned to use his wry humor as a counteractive. Notice how he will parry a sharp thrust by anticipating it and putting himself down ever so gently? He has also developed this into the fine art of counter-attack and can both disarm and disengage the attacker without causing hostility. (In his film *Manhattan*, for example, Diane Keaton starts out being his antagonist and ends up being his lover). Allen's self-deprecation carries the kernel of love that comes from how well he understands himself and the human condition. It is not self-destructive. Rather, it is self-protective.

There can be a very moving quality to some expressions of self-deprecation. My heart went out not long ago to a marvelous drunk who, on one of the coldest days of the year, was standing on the street without an overcoat. His ungloved hand was extended and he had a lovely, sweet smile on his face. No one stopped to give him money, and the only thing I heard him say as I passed was, "I'll tell you one good thing about me—I ain't cold."

I loved that man for finding one good thing to tell about himself.

The sweetness in the way he said it made me feel like laughing and crying at the same time. He made me feel a great tenderness.

We are forgiving toward those for whom we feel tenderness.

And you need to feel tenderness toward yourself, especially when you are depressed. Before anyone else's, you need your own understanding.

Try what I call "taking turns." By a process of psychological alchemy, use this formula to turn anger and self-disgust into tenderness and understanding.

Turn your self-disgust into self-deprecation.
Turn self-deprecation into laughing at yourself.
Turn laughing at yourself into inhibiting your self-criticism.
Turn inhibiting your self-criticism into tenderness.
Turn tenderness into understanding.

Turn your anger at yourself into anger at your inactivity.
Turn anger at your inactivity into resolve.
Turn resolve into planning.
Turn planning into action.
Turn action into self-appreciation.
Turn self-appreciation into tenderness.
Turn tenderness into understanding.

When you feel tenderly toward yourself and when you understand yourself you do not feel depressed.

Rodgers and Hart wrote a wonderful song called "Glad to Be Unhappy." The advice it offers is a very good prescription. The song begins by suggesting that you look at yourself, and comments:

If you had a sense of humor,
You'd laugh to beat the band!

This wise observation is followed by a description of unrequited love. The song relates the behavior of the "fool for love" who rushes in, but still doesn't get his/her heart's desire. And then, the unhappy lover in the song decides:

But for someone you adore,
It's a pleasure to be sad.

And reaches the conclusion: "I'm so unhappy—but oh—so —glad!" I like this song because "fools rush in"—is the action you need to take.

"I'm so unhappy—but oh—so—glad—" is *not* the sentiment of a depressed person!

So when it comes to singing the blues, let me remind you that I am not talking about eliminating all sadness and all sorrow from life. I am not saying that you will never know a moment's unhappiness again if you sample my nostrums. What I am saying is that depression is not unhappiness. Depression is not sadness or sorrow. Depression is depression.

Depression is largely a habit. Why not kick the habit?

CHAPTER 6

Risking, Gambling, Spending Money, and Going out on a Limb or How *Not* to Go Broke During Your Depression

I have touched briefly on the risk element in two contexts: risking pain by swimming around in the midst of life, and risking pride, feelings, or money in investments (of all sorts). I think they are related. I think you need to be able to risk not only for the stimulation which works to block entertainment depression, but because by being willing to take a chance on yourself, you put yourself on call for the best that's in you. And by so doing, you work against habitual depression.

As recreation, gambling may be the most popular form of risk-taking—unless you want to lump all sports activities together, in which case we'd probably have a tie. But behind sports participation, sports spectating, gambling, or any form of competition, the element of risk is at play. You, yourself, however, are the most important thing there is to bet on.

If you take a quick look at where we evolved from, you'll recognize that our species had to do a good deal of scary stuff constantly in order to survive. There were all those big, toothy, and clawy *others* competing for space and food; there were the incomprehensibly huge heavens threatening and scowling and flinging thunder and lightning bolts of flashing fire; there were lashing winds and burning sun and torrents of water—and, of course, we had each other to contend with. So we really had to be a scrappy bunch to last. In fact, we had to have a taste for it!

To sum up my anthropological survey of the last three million years or so, I will simply add that as we became citified and dandified, we had to find something to do with all the feistiness—so we got to gambling and sporting around and fisticuffing to keep our risk-taking juices flowing in a safe, ritualized fashion. Because, leading back to the beginning of my circumlocution, *we need to risk*. I'm not at all sure but that war isn't one of the outcomes when the rituals wear thin. Desmond Morris notes in *The Human Zoo:* ". . . it is intriguing to notice how many sports and hobbies involve an element of ritualized aggression, over and above simple competitiveness."

Fear

One of the indirect causes of depression is fear. It shows itself in the way we seek approval from others, in the way we slavishly follow convention, in the way we go with the crowd rather than choose what suits us individually.

Let's make this assumption: every sane human being (or animal of any species) experiences fear at some time in life. It's part of your safety equipment. The sensation of fear does certain things to your body chemically which affect you physically—your heart pounds, you break into a sweat, and so on. Since we no longer have brontosaurs or pterodactyls flying around, and have taken instead to living in very "civilized" surroundings, our fear mechanisms have adapted to new beasts of prey: your boss may very well have become your brontosaur (he *has* been putting on a bit of heft lately), or your business competitor is fighting you for that bit of worm you're both after. Fine. This is nothing new. And, as Konrad Lorenz said about the lioness stalking her prey in the jungle, "She's not exhibiting aggression, she's just shopping." However, we still think there is something slightly unsavory about our taste for risk and our penchant for competition. "It isn't nice. Ladies and gentlemen don't do it—particularly ladies." Well I don't agree! That lioness is a *real* lady!

One of the things that happened to us when we adapted to city lights was that we got overrefined. There were so many new and bizarre threats to deal with (the pterodactyls look like canaries by comparison) that it seemed better and safer to become passive in the face of them and blend in with the crowd. The necessity of living in a crowd promoted passivity as a virtue and reinforced the conviction that it was altogether a good thing to be retiring. But retreat wasn't all that easy. The essential mechanisms that let us survive the beasts of prey and the assaults from an unknown heaven were still there, part of our natural endowment; still operational, still serving us in our up-to-date survival kit. And that's when all those fun sublimations began—the "modern" ways of letting the risk-taking juices flow: the thrill at the roulette table or the track, playing the stock market, killing off the competition, screaming at the butcher, standing too near the subway tracks, driving too fast . . . and so on.

My theory is that those of us who either never found or never acknowledged healthy, exuberant sublimations for our innate aggressions beat ourselves down into a too-passive quietude. When this happens, fear increases and becomes transmuted inwardly into depression—you hate your fear and you hate yourself for having it. You're afraid of not being approved of, liked, wanted; you're afraid of failure or success, compromise or obstinacy, trying too hard or too little, being too conventional or too eccentric, pushing too hard or not hard enough. You constantly test your posture in the reflection you see in someone else's eyes. And, because there is always a distortion in that mirror, you constantly attempt to adjust yourself to meet an outside image of what you think you should be. All because of fear—fear of not being accepted, not being loved.

Ask yourself—what would be the worst thing that could happen if—?

Almost invariably the worst thing you can dream of to fear isn't that bad!

Once I had to audition for a singing job with an opera company. I will tell you that I wasn't just afraid; I was completely panicked. I was terrified. I was so scared that my own fear was incomprehensible to me. The day before the audition I was pacing around like a terrified animal. "Why are you so afraid?" I kept asking myself. "What terrible thing do you think could happen?" But there was no answer to be had. I didn't know what I was afraid of or why. Along about dinnertime I decided I had to do something, so I called my doctor and told him the story. He phoned in a prescription to my druggist. (You've got to know how unusual this was when I tell you that in my whole life, I don't think I've taken any kind of sedative or tranquilizer [except aspirin] more than three or four times.)

I picked up the sedative and went back home to pace. Finally I began to ask myself a few more questions: "What is the worst thing that could happen?" I inquired and considered the possibilities in my imagination. Living through it in my mind, I saw that the worst thing was that I would make a complete and utter ass of myself. "So what if you do?" I answered myself. "In certain circumstances, it's a privilege to make a fool of yourself!" It became increasingly clear that this was only part of what I feared.

Continuing to chisel away at it, I went into my bedroom and lay down in the dark. Per my doctor's advice I had decided to take one of the sedatives before going to sleep and the second one when I got up in the morning.

Painstakingly I tried to sort out exactly what I was feeling. I examined the nature of my fear—what was it like? What could I compare it to? I suddenly pictured it as an anthropomorphic demon who resided inside me, complete with leer and sharp teeth. I knew we were in a struggle for possession of my premises, even my life—for if I gave in to my demon of fear now, I would never be able to sing in public. Since I wanted that more than anything, my whole life was really on the line. I also knew that my demon would not stop with stagefright. Oh no! If I lost this one,

I would soon find fear demons trespassing on other lawns. I had one of those moments of clarity that comes a few times in your life when you see and know that you are in the middle of wrestling with one of the great issues of your life. Yes. If I lost this one, I was lost to fear for good. This is what I thought as I lay there writhing. Writhing and *thinking*.

Then I stopped picturing my demon and began to focus on the base of my fear. Again, in my mind's eye, I walked out on the stage and faced the music. What would happen at that precise moment? Would I run off the stage like a child? Would I be able to get any sound out whatsoever? Would I sing so badly that they would laugh?

As I lived through that moment in my imagination, it suddenly came to me that the reason I was so terrified was that *I didn't know what was going to happen*. Then, in a flash of insight, I realized that I had been assuming that the battle I was facing would take place out there on that stage in front of everybody! In public! *That's* what I was afraid of! The humiliation of being a fool in public. Immediately, I realized that the real battle was taking place right there and then in that dark room in my own bed all by myself. By the time I walked out on the stage the next morning, it would have already been won or lost. In fact, the outcome was being decided right there and then in my bedroom.

I cannot convey the relief I felt then, for it was at that very moment that I won the battle. I knew I would not be afraid onstage. I knew I had won. I stopped searching frantically for an escape from going through with what I had decided to do. I went through it successfully in my mind and had complete confidence that I would go through it successfully onstage.

The dénouement came the next morning when I went to the audition. I never sang better in my life. I had known that this would be the case before I stepped out on the stage. And I never experienced that kind of mindless stage-fright panic again.

Whenever you go out on a limb, you're laying it on the line. Taking a chance with your money in gambling is a cinch compared to risking your pride, your ego, your image, and your self-esteem. In the subterranean depths of your being, you know you have to risk because it's part of being alive. *Ergo,* when you are too afraid to risk, you hate yourself for cowering in the back of a dark closet, and you have the sure knowledge that you are not totally alive. How can you be when you're so scared? This is what downers are made of.

Life is scary. Living is dangerous. Practically every minute you're alive there is something to threaten you on some level. You cannot completely avoid danger, no matter how much you hide. Paranoids of the world hearken—everything *is* after you!

But then, everything is after everybody. We're all in it together. You're not singled out because of your big, shiny eyes. It's not fair or unfair—it just is. So why not make the best of it and make the best of who and what you are?

Use the Risk Element!

Now we get to the fun part. If you accept that the fear mechanism is there for a good reason, you can figure out what to do with it. You can put it in your bag of nostrums for fighting your depressions—particularly the entertainment and habitual varieties.

If you recognize your own fear behavior and want to break out of it, begin with what's easiest—

RISK YOUR MONEY:

- Go out and play bridge (or golf) at a club for high stakes (medium high).
- Or get yourself invited to a serious poker game, if that's more your thing, where you could conceivably lose half a week's salary (no more than half).
- Spend ten bucks at your local bingo parlor.
- Take a walk around your favorite shopping area and buy yourself something you really want but don't need (pay for it by skipping lunch for a month).

97

After you've warmed up with a few risks involving money, you're ready to graduate to the more meaningful kind.

RISK LOOKING LIKE A FOOL:

- Call up a guy or gal you had a terrific thing for a couple of years back and find out how it's going with him or her.
- Do something you've always wanted to do, such as writing a letter to the editor of your local paper on some matter you feel strongly about—and sign your name.
- Join the theatre group in your neighborhood and go out for a part in the next production.
- Don't tip the waiter when you've had bad service (and tell him why nicely).
- Write to your favorite TV quiz show and see if you can get on as a contestant.

RISK SHOWING YOUR TRUE FEELINGS:

- Tell somebody off when you're angry (and I mean off!). Let it all out at the person who made you sore—just be sure they've earned it.
- Tell a friend or acquaintance you admire them and why.
- Tell someone you love them and in what ways.
- Disagree with someone who is in a position to help or hinder you (*if* you really feel disagreement on some point).
- Ask someone whom you respect for corroboration of something they say that you find difficult to believe.
- Tell your friends something good about yourself that you did recently.

RISK BEING VULNERABLE:

- If you feel you deserve it, ask for a raise.
- Tell someone who cares about you what you're afraid of and why.

- Let someone who can understand see you cry.
- Trust someone not to disapprove of you by telling something about yourself you feel ashamed of.
- Share confidences with a friend about your Achilles' heel.

Risks are "openings up"—and if you think of them in opposition to "closings down," I think you'll see my point.

The secret of risk taking is that you must not look for anything in return for your opening up. When you tell someone you admire or like him it must be without strings —freely given—so that it will be gladly received. The purpose is not to have your recipient turn around on the spot and rub your back in return. What you get out of it is far more important—*it will feel good to you.* You will feel good about the other person and you will end up feeling good about yourself. Once you develop an attitude of mind that looks for things to like, admire, love, and feel good about, finding them will become habitual. It doesn't matter whether you begin by looking for what to feel good about in the other person or in yourself (it may be easier to start with the other person)—it works both ways, in a reciprocal fashion; the more you find to feel good about, the less you will have to feel bad about.

You can teach yourself to risk, to dare, to trust being yourself, and to trust others with yourself. You will become more emboldened after each successful step, so that you will be able to risk something a little bit scarier each time. Start with the easiest things for you, and devise your own campaign in terms of increasing the challenge. Don't worry about the final, most difficult ones first (that's the best way to scare yourself out of the whole endeavor). There's no time limit. You're not in a race with anyone, and no one says you have to do all of your assigned openers within any prescribed time period. I think you will *want* to risk a little more each time, because it's exciting and because you'll like yourself better and better as you're doing it.

Remember, set up a gradual progression of steps; make it an easy ascent so that you can adjust to the altitude as you go along. Don't try to do everything in a day and a half—please!

Like walking the tightrope that's stretched across the abyss, you should practice close to the edge until you become quite good at it. That way if you lose your balance the first three dozen times, you can still grab hold of the ledge and break your fall.

When you get the hang of risking, you'll scoot across like an expert. And, as a shrink I know once said, "The safest place to be is out on a limb."

CHAPTER 7

Short-Term *Versus* Long-Term Measures

I have mentioned the existence of both short-term and long-term measures, and I think it's time to talk about when and how to use which. As in banking, short-term notes are designed to meet your pressing needs of the moment, and you must pay a fairly high rate of interest for them. Your long-term needs must be met by careful investments, which pay you high dividends.

Short-term measures are meant to deal with crises or emergencies, or to tide you over a rough patch. Long-term measures are big, ongoing commitments that are woven into the fabric of your life. Sometimes you need to take out both at the same time in order to get dramatic, fast relief while waiting for the slower, more permanent help to develop. They do not supplant each other, and you should not be confused about what you are seeking from each. When they are used in conjunction, they support and further each other's benefits, and the sum of their combined usefulness to you is greater than their separate benefits.

The rule of thumb is this: whenever you can, employ your long-term measure first. If you do not achieve sufficient relief (some long-terms *can* give fast relief) then add on your short-termer. By starting with the long-termer, you

101

lay the groundwork for a future payoff while you are getting your temporary help. And you will receive compounded interest from it, just as you do with a savings account.

Most short-term measures are based on distraction. Get your mind off it, think about something else, don't dwell on it—are call letters that announce a short-term measure. The common garden variety distraction is readily available in all forms of show biz, sports, hobbies, travel, games, books, and so on. The businessman's Broadway show is notoriously light becaue it is intended to be a distraction, not an art form. One of the major differences between entertainment and art is that entertainment is designed to be a distraction; art is not.

There are times when you are so down that you cannot stand even to think about long-term measures. When this is the case, you must find relief before you can do anything to help yourself on a more profound level. The reason getting drunk is the most common form of self-treatment among depressives is because, as Freud said, "A change of mood is the most precious thing that alcohol achieves for mankind." As a short-term measure, the appeal of alcohol is that it temporarily cheers you up, or calms you down, or acts to change whatever you're feeling to something different. What is important is the change. You can achieve relief through every day remedies such as taking a hot bath (changes your temperature), taking a walk (changes your scenery), or drinking fruit juice (changes your blood sugar level).

Since depression is delicately balanced, even a tiny change can be salubrious. Sometimes the change can be as small as a smile or the mere presence of another human being. This is why distractions work so well.

The fastest and surest method of obtaining quick relief is not (contrary to what many depressives feel) alcohol. It is talking to a sympathetic person. Throughout this book, you will find references to talking and listening and the roles that both play in dealing with depression. Successful talking and successful listening are so important that I have considered different aspects in various contexts. But in general, let me say that the discharge of emotional energy that talking offers, with or without tears, is cathartic. By enabling you to get rid of some of the charge, you achieve the change you need. The more you can bare (bear) your soul, the more inner tension and pressure you will discharge and the more relief you will feel. A tensed wire is tight. A loose wire is relaxed. Anything that relaxes you will automatically offer a short-term benefit.

Shrinks are the best listeners for this purpose, whether or not you have real and true friends. When you are in an acute state of depression, a therapist can offer a variety of short-term "crisis intervention" measures. What intervenes (comes between you and your depression) is the human, caring presence, which offers you the opportunity to release your internal pressure by literally "airing" it. Airing is preferable to drowning it or burying it—by far.

The object is first to get through the acute phase in one piece and then go on from there. "Airing" your problem with a good shrink provides long-term benefits in addition to the immediate relief—*the moment of crisis can be one of great and fruitful insight.* Nothing is more revealing than terrific pain *if* it is used correctly to probe the depths. A skillful shrink, by going through the crisis with you, can help you guide the knife of insight to the source of the pain and help you excise it. Hard-hearted as this may sound, this gut-racking, steely-eyed confrontation is a better alternative than easy distraction and quick surcease of pain. So, if you can possibly stand it, rather than using distraction for short-term relief, you're better off using the crisis for a good look into your private hell. You'll feel worse before you feel better, but the view is fantastic; and you'll feel better—in a better way—sooner than you think.

I did manage to look into the heart of the matter once when I was at the bottom of the pit (which is the peak of the pain). I was feeling very down on myself, feeling that I was a failure in everything I attempted: work, love, friendship—everything. The event that brought me to this point was the ending of a love affair, but I saw it as just one more thing in a long line of messups in my life. I was talking about the agonizing pain of failure, which was always with me and which my shrink had never gotten to the bottom of. From outside, I appeared to have had a normally successful life, yet nothing ever satisfied me. Nothing I ever did was enough. I did many things which impressed other people, but I couldn't accept compliments or appreciation for my talents. Significantly, I felt I had never done anything that was good enough. Since I had been singing in public from the time I was eleven years old, it was easy to leap onto my mother as the cause of my malcontent. Time and again my shrink had probed the issue, looking for evidence of a mother who could not be satisfied. Time and time again I had said helplessly that my mother had been more than satisfied with me and with what I had accomplished. No matter how many times I told my shrink that in my mother's eyes I was a success, somehow the question remained, and my feelings of failure and dissatisfaction with myself were unresolved.

On this particular occasion, for some reason which I can no longer recall, I brought up a very old grief that had caused me incredible pain—the death of a beloved sister (she died when I was about three) at the age of sixteen and the death of a beloved brother who was killed in war at the age of twenty-five. Of all my siblings, I had adored these two. And the terrible sense of loss which I suffered as a result of these early deaths hardly compares to the devastation wreaked on my mother.

In bringing up that experience on this particular day, I suddenly made the connection that I had never been able to make before. All my life I had wanted to live for *three* people, accomplish for three. I had childishly wanted to do so much and be so many great things so that I could make up for my mother's loss. It was not in her mind (she had no idea of what I was trying to do) but unconsciously, it had always been in mine. For this reason nothing was ever sufficient. How could it be? I was only one person, not three.

As I made this connection for the first time in my life, the pain was excruciating. Of course I had failed; no wonder I was never satisfied by my own accomplishments. I wept almost hysterically, but through the intense pain, the sights I saw were so revealing that after a while, I began to feel easier. I left my session that day with a great sense of optimism because I'd had such a penetrating insight into the real core of one of the biggest problems of my life. I felt good in a way I had never felt good before—I felt that my future could now hold success for me instead of failure.

So, just as there is always something to feel depressed about, there's always something to feel good about.

At this point I am tempted to write down all the optimist-pessimist stories I know, but you've probably heard most of them. I'll content myself with reminding you of the little optimist who found horse droppings in his Christmas stocking and squealed with great excitement and joy, "Oh boy! Santa Claus brought me a pony for Christmas. All I have to do is find it!"

That, of course, is all any of us have to do.

Returning to the subject of measures, let's talk about some of the destructive ways people distract themselves.

Sex

Ordinary people do not speak of sex as a measure, but many use it as such. It would be interesting to do a study of all the things people use sex for besides sex, but for now I'll confine myself to the use of sex as a measure for beating depression. Let me say first that it's chancy at best and dangerous at worst. The danger lies in the overwhelming likelihood of having it backfire and leave you twice as depressed as you were before you went to bed.

Sex is the most fun, the most rewarding, the most joyous and happiness-provoking when it is free, spontaneous, and full of loving—which you already know. So it beats me why so many people pursue sex when they are tied up in knots, deliberately looking for out-and-out distraction, miserable, and full of self-loathing. You want to bet on a sure thing? Bet you'll louse it up every time you try to have sex when you're feeling depressed.

Here's what happens. You're feeling down. You don't like yourself. You're single. You want to feel better about yourself, so you immediately start looking for somebody else who thinks you're nifty. "A-ha," you cry, "nothing

105

like a little score to take my mind off what a zero I feel like."

Oh yeah?

Next, you find some poor unsuspecting soul. You raise your eyebrows five or six times (à la Groucho Marx) in comic imitation of sexual arousal although we both know you're not aroused. Your poor dumb victim bites. Comes the bed scene: you can't get anything up! Not your self-esteem. Not your spirits. Not your hopes. Not your enthusiasm. And certainly not your libido!

Now you really have got something to feel down about. "I can't even do *that* anymore," you say to yourself (as if *that* were a mechanical feat like snapping your fingers). And the final blow to your ego comes when your partner "understands" and says something kind like, "Oh you're just tired, honey . . ." or, "It doesn't matter." There's nothing like "understanding" to wash your prowess right down the drain. Worse still (if you are female), you fake it and your partner doesn't catch on. Try *that* for making yourself feel like instant bread crumbs.

Or you're married. You go through the same routine as the single person, figuring that if somebody besides your mate thinks you're nifty, it will take your mind off how little you think of yourself. Or it will serve your mate right for not making you feel nifty. You've got a better than fair chance to end up feeling guilty rather than nifty, and guilt is a frequent precursor of depression. Result: using sex to relieve depression has backfired.

Suppose you're married and you're depressed and your mate wants sex but you're not interested. "I'll go through the motions," you say to yourself. So you try. You turn yourself into an acquiescent body and lie there out of obligation. You do this enough times and a lot of other problems start to develop (which can, by the way, distract you from your depression) Another backfire: now you've lost the pleasure of having sex with your mate. If you want holding and being held, don't be afraid to tell your partner that it's comfort you want, not sex. When you feel comforted, the chances are good that your interest in sex will return. It is disturbing how many women endure sex to get comfort.

106

Then there is the twisted technique that involves using the person's feelings as a diversion.

A short toss around the four-poster isn't enough of a distraction for some sad souls. They need to have everybody fall in love with them—either in the form of multiple lovers or merely multiple flirtations.

This type of person is like what in physics is called a black hole or a black star. In astronomy, a "black hole" or a "black star" occurs when a star gets very old and collapses in on itself, becoming an enormous, gaping negative hole in the sky that devours all the positive energy it can gobble up.

You can always recognize a human black star by the trail he or she leaves. In this regard, our human black star resembles a comet. It appears quite glamorous from a distance, but when analyzed closely, it turns out that its dazzling, flashy tail is actually the debris of former lovers who burn up when they hit the down-to-earth atmosphere. Black stars are never wholly satisfied or happy except for one small evanescent second *just before* they capture the next heavenly body. This is because the only thing that makes them happy is the challenge of trying to attain the unattainable. Our black stars never got enough love as kids, and now there aren't enough lovers in the universe to gobble up. Nothing can satisfy them.

Having people fall in love with you whether you're married or single, and acting out or fantasizing the fable of falling in love, when used as a distraction for depression, will inevitably ricochet—it will come back and slam you in the head every time, leaving you in a deeper depression than before. You reinforce your feeling of failure in love again and again—and by so doing, you reinforce your feeling that you are basically unlovable and unworthy of love. The truth is that *basically you are lovable*—it's the surface that's giving you trouble. You're using love superficially, not basically, and that's the problem.

Now that I have convinced you that using sex and love as short-term measures is not the best idea, let's go into what *is* the best idea.

The black star has got to discover first of all that love is *loving,* not being loved.

Being loved is somebody else's loving! It's nice if someone bestows it on you, but it's still their loving, not yours. The trouble with you is not that you're unloved, but that you're unloving.

What can you do about that?

First, admit it—because I'll be willing to bet that the minute you read the line above about not being loving, you thought to yourself, "I *am* loving."

Okay, maybe you are—but you are not loving enough. The reason I know you are not is that you certainly aren't loving yourself enough. And by loving yourself, I do not mean pamper, indulge, spoil, cater to, dote on, or be obsessed with—I mean *love.*

Begin by realizing that loving is a big subject. It covers a lot of ground. Objects to love are myriad. Ways of loving are manifold. There are enough things out there to love, if you look for all the varieties, to satisfy the largest, blackest, gapingest black star in the universe. The bind that limits you is the idea that you can only satisfy your need for love by falling in love or being fallen in love with. As a matter of fact, until you get to the point where you are doing the real kind of loving, falling isn't going to get you anywhere but down.

So, for the time being, please do not pick out a human being as your object. Not just yet. Set yourself up with an entire catalogue of what there is to love in the world (and out of it) and begin to practice loving everything from *A* to *Z.* Actually make yourself a list and fill in as many items under each letter as you can think of that could be lovable. Then . . . go to it! The more love you feel for anything, the more love you will have.

Do not, repeat *not,* seek objects to return your love— that's not the point! Skip pets, too, for the moment, because pets are too often used as substitutes for humans. Pets should be loved for themselves, not as a replacement for humans—and until you learn the difference, you may use them for a copout. After you have learned to walk the one-way street of love, you'll find that two-way traffic comes naturally.

So, rather than using love as a short-term measure, fall in love with loving. It could change your entire life. After you fall in love with loving, sex will take care of itself for you—and I don't mean short-term!

Back in chapter two, I promised you a whole list of Modes of Fleeing which you can use consciously as short-term measures when you need them. There are, of course, lots of ways to flee. You can flee very effectively without moving a muscle. If something with nasty little sharp teeth is snapping at your heels, you may climb a tree. Or you may not answer the telephone. Or you may be "busy" all the time. By being socially tied up, you can flee from something you want to avoid without moving a muscle.

At this very moment, millions of people are engaged in fleeing all over the roads and sidewalks of the world. Jogging can be a very healthy way to flee—and if you acknowledge that aspect of it out loud, it's twice as healthy.

If you know someone who is so constantly on the move that he gives you motion sickness, chances are this person is fleeing. A sure sign of depression at the heels is when your lover's idea (or yours) of a really great weekend together is to get into a car and drive, drive, drive. This is not to say that wanting to go for a ride in the country is automatically fleeing (that's sloppy filing)—but be wary when the only thing you want to do for a getaway is get away.

You might want to practice spotting fleeing patterns in your friends and acquaintances as they try to outrun depression. Look over the Modes of Fleeing and see who you know who fits into each one. How many do you do yourself? Once you recognize them, you can *choose* to flee by design. The short-term benefits make excellent temporary nostrums for relieving the acute stage of your downer.

The Modes of Fleeing that follow are those things we do which can have both regular benefits as well as special benefits when we use them for fleeing. We should be aware of both sets of benefits and elect to use them for fleeing—*consciously*—when we see fit. The dangers (aside from the obvious physical ones inherent in some of the more abusive activities) occur when you use any Mode of Fleeing *unconsciously* for its special benefits. This unconscious use facilitates an avoidance of your depression, and by so doing, prevents you from coming to grips with the cause.

Modes of Fleeing	Regular Benefits	Special Benefits When Used For Fleeing
Jogging, Biking, Ice-skating, Skiing	make you healthy and chic; firm your muscles and keep your weight down; offer you a way of meeting people; give you topics of social conversation.	tire you physically so you sleep better; make you feel you are doing something that is good for you; make you feel more attractive.
Driving a car	gets you out in the fresh air; puts you in touch with nature.	offers you a sense of control over something; gives you a feeling of power; forces you to concentrate on basics like not running into another car; is an extension of jogging which enables you to move farther and faster away.
Overwork	helps you get ahead and earn more money;	makes you feel important and self-sacrificing;

Modes of Fleeing	Regular Benefits	Special Benefits When Used For Fleeing
(Overwork)	scores extra points with the boss.	takes your mind off the inner demons and puts it on constructive thoughts; uses up energy that you would have worried with; is something to do when you can't sleep; is a form of addiction which gives a pleasant high.
Multiple Lovers	sharpen your imagination and inventiveness by having to get out of "situations."	keep the phone ringing; force you to use your brain constantly to prevent one from finding out about the others; exhaust you physically; create so many conflicting demands that you do not have to consider making a commitment or forming a deep relationship; are good for your ego; make you feel attractive.

Modes of Fleeing	Regular Benefits	Special Benefits When Used For Fleeing
Getting drunk	makes you feel free and daring and lets you be silly, morose, or angry instead of repressing those things; offers you a change of mood.	puts you to sleep for a while; garbles your conversation so you don't have to make sense or communicate; gives you a terrific headache and/or stomachache, which puts everything into perspective as to what's really important; makes everyone else seem attractive.
Eating	is a means of social intercourse; gives you a creative outlet in gourmet cooking or appreciation.	gives instant gratification; is a form of reward or consolation; can act as a blocking agent by preoccupying your thoughts.
Smoking	offers an outlet for nervous energy; gives you something to do with your hands.	gives instant oral gratification; makes you feel grown-up or sophisticated; lets you identify with a virile image like the Marlboro man.

Modes of Fleeing	Regular Benefits	Special Benefits When Used For Fleeing
Sleeping	lets you get both psychic and physical rest.	brings oblivion; prevents you from having to do anything; is a mild form of paralysis which offers an escape from awareness.
Games and Spectator Sports	give you an opportunity to compete directly or indirectly; are stimulating and exciting.	give you something to root for without taking responsibility; get your hostility juices flowing outward.
Entertainments, Movies, TV, Shows	let you involve yourself in other people's stories, dreams, and agonies; make you laugh or cry; stimulate your imagination.	let you identify with heroes and heroines; free you from self-absorption; keep your thoughts from turning inward.
Travel	exposes you on the broadest scale to external ideas; takes you completely out of yourself, your culture and even your times; gives you new sensations; expands your	diverts you from focusing on yourself; gives you a sense of cleverness from coping with strange situations; is the ultimate extension of jogging.

Modes of Fleeing	Regular Benefits	Special Benefits When Used For Fleeing
(Travel)	ability to cope by presenting you with frequent inconveniences; teaches you to improvise and make do.	
Reading	is informative, enlightening and educational; broadens your horizons; keeps you in touch with your times; stretches your imagination; contributes to your store of small talk.	transforms you into your ideal image of yourself; allows you to meet and master all situations; shows you other people's insides without exposing you to them; lets you become anyone you ever wanted to be.
Art and Creative Endeavor	are the most thoroughly absorbing activities yet devised; make you lose all self-consciousness; encourage you to lose your inhibitions; offer your imagination and originality the fullest outlet; contribute to	give you enormous anxiety and enormous fulfillment in the same package; call for great expenditure of psychic energy, which exhausts you; drain you of emotions; serve as perfect excuses for unconventional

Modes of Fleeing	Regular Benefits	Special Benefits When Used For Fleeing
(Art and Creative Endeavor)	your élan, panache and brio; turn other people on.	behavior; give you a glamorous and sexy aura; help you appear mysterious and inaccessible; can be used to camouflage anything.
Shopping	uses up energy; accomplishes chores.	gives you an immediate outlet for experiencing and expressing frustration; makes you feel good because of the money you save or spend; is a form of jogging that doesn't require special shoes; gives you a goal when you have to return what you bought.
House cleaning	heightens your pride and promotes your sense of shelter security; encourages you to entertain; gets you to throw things away.	uses up energy while giving you a sense of accomplishment.

115

Modes of Fleeing	Regular Benefits	Special Benefits When Used For Fleeing
Gardening and Home-Improvement Projects	let you use your hands and brain at the same time; give you things to show for your effort; improve your surroundings.	are good for your image; develop calluses to display to your friends.
Courses at the Y	help discipline your mind; teach you new skills; lead to new perspectives, achievements; and appreciations, help you meet new people; keep you interested and interesting; are well-rounding.	give you a place to go weeknights; make you seem earnest; take you out of your limited set of activities; make you feel constructive.
Beauty Parlors and Barber Shops	express a healthy interest in your looks and ego.	let you be the center of attention; let you be soothed, patted, stroked without becoming emotionally involved; simulate mating and grooming behavior.

The thing to remember about fleeing is that it is only bad when you don't know you're doing it, or when you do it constantly instead of dealing with the problems that cause you to want to do it. But as I pointed out earlier, the things we use to flee with, by, or through are the very things that have much intrinsic value for us as regular parts of our lives.

The Regular Benefits can be used by you, just as the Special Benefits when used for fleeing can help you to distract yourself *consciously* when the need arises. Distraction is not a bad thing—it has its time and place. When it is used as a short-term measure, it should be either preceded or followed by a long-term measure.

Any short-term measure, taken alone, will sooner or later lose its effectiveness—you can only successfully distract yourself for a limited period of time. Otherwise distraction becomes *self-delusion*, and you become depressed about that.

If you employ the temporary nostrums *for what they are* while you are waiting for the results of your long-term measures to come in, you will gain relief without feeling that you have avoided the real issue. You'll have used the short-termer as it was intended to be used—to help you get up off the floor, or the bed as the case may be.

The key to the successful use of any short-term measure is your *conscious awareness and choice*. Short-term measures should never to be used to replace or ignore the long term. They are both valuable numbers in your repertoire, but serve completely different purposes. *You* determine what you need. *You* select the measure that you feel will help you.

With the Down Comforter, you can bank on collecting interest on your long-term investments and take out a short-term note (if you need to) at the same time.

117

CHAPTER 8

How to Choose Ways
to Be a *Little* Self-Destructive
or Safety Valves and
Shock Treatments

If you suffer from habitual depression you may argue that —like garlic and being pregnant—there is no such thing as being a *little* self-destructive. I grant you that I could have called this chapter, "How to Choose Minor Ways to Be Self-Destructive," for there *are* major and minor leagues in self-destructiveness, and both leagues are comprised of different clubs.

Self-destructiveness is totally negative behavior. We all do some of it sometime in life. No one recommends it. However, as I pointed out in describing the opposites that are characteristic of depression, it is possible to use the negative to achieve its opposite—in this case, positive, self-constructive behavior.

It is my view that habitual depression, being the most difficult to overcome, will not yield readily to ordinary or conventional methods. Habitual depression calls for strong medicine. Therefore, I am going to recommend what no one recommends—I am going to recommend a "weaning" approach: a substitution of lesser evils for greater evils, eventually leading to no evils, and finally the replacement of destructive mental habits with constructive mental habits.

Keep in mind that the long range goal is eventually to eliminate *both major and minor* forms (clubs) of self-destructiveness. Mental habits dictate behavior, therefore every club you're a member of is exacting dues, and this is one instance when your membership privileges are nil!

Begin by looking over the following line-up of major league forms of self-destructive mental habits and identifying the clubs you belong in. Put a check mark next to each.

Major League Clubs of Self-Destructive Mental Habits	Bad Effects (Membership Dues)
Worrying	Increases self-doubt, interferes with positive action, is ulcer-provoking, blocks pleasure and enjoyment; leads to approval-seeking, guarding and withholding from others.
Misdirecting Anger	Causes self-hatred, self-loathing; hostility, sarcasm, snappishness, and attacking; displacement of negative feelings to innocent parties.
Feeling Guilty	Motivates self-punishment, self-deprivation, compulsions, and obsessions; causes impotence, ambivalence, and torments to those who love you.
Being Hyper-Critical	Leads to self-deprecation and low self-esteem, fault-finding, undervaluing, negating, and putting on the defensive.

Major League Clubs of Self-Destructive Mental Habits	Bad Effects (Membership Dues)
Being Afraid	Brings about self-distrust, anxiety, inhibitions, timidity, and inability to risk; distrust and withdrawal from others, suspicion and shunning.
Being Rigid	Causes inability to perceive alternatives, paralysis, entrapment of self and others; rejection of everything unfamiliar; invulnerability, inaccessibility.
Having Unreal Expectations	Brings about delusory self-image, self-condemnation, unreal demands, paralyzing perfectionism, chronic disappointment, letdown, never being pleased by or having anything be enough; never knowing real satisfaction.
Hypochondria	Punishes your body with actual physical discomforts and illnesses; interferes with a realistic view of your abilities and disabilities; is costly in time, energy, and money spent on doctors and medicines; can lead to chronic illness and chronic impairment of functions.

Next, look over the following list of minor league forms of self-destructive behavior or mental habits and check the ones you habitually indulge in. (If you don't like the minors I have drawn up, by all means line up some different ones of your own.)

Minor League Clubs of Self-Destructive Behavior or Mental Habits	Bad Effects (Membership Dues)
Asociality	Makes you seem snooty, reclusive, or withdrawn, closes you off from outside influences and stimulation; brings about avoidance and rejection.
Audacity	Displays aggressiveness and lack of restraint, encourages overpursuit and pesty behavior; results in challenging, defying, and competing with others.
Outrageousness	Makes you seem kooky, coarse, gross, or stupid, eccentric, unconventional, insulting, shocking, embarrassing, puzzling, and shaming.
Freakishness and Bizarre Entertainments	Weirdness, craziness, alienation, and distortion of reality; makes people nervous, scared, estranged, disgusted.
Self-preoccupation	Is desensitizing and puts you out of touch, reduces outside contact, causes loss of interest from others, makes you boring.
Carelessness and Indifference	Causes loss of self-respect, disinvolvement, disconnection; increases despair, encourages you to give up the struggle, makes others lose respect for you and induces indifference.

121

Minor League Clubs of Self-Destructive Behavior or Mental Habits	Bad Effects (Membership Dues)
Avoidance	Prevents you from confronting or grappling with your problems, keeps you out of touch and out of reach, disguises your true feelings, makes it impossible for anyone to have a real relationship with you.

Now, with a view toward farming out some of your majors to the minors where they will do less damage, write down the unchecked, minor league clubs of self-destructive behavior that are open to you. Proceed to make your selections. You will be transferring the *checked* behavior habits on the major league list to the *unchecked* ones on the minor league list.

Since this will be your first day of the "weaning" process, you should experience considerable trouble in getting yourself to accept the new minor league self-destructive habit(s) you're switching to . . . after all, if you've been Worrying excessively for years and you have selected Audacity to switch to, you're bound to feel awkward the first few dozen times you bust loose and let the devil take the high road. But if you let yourself *use* Audacity by design, it will knock the hell out of Worrying. The same thing is true if you've been Misdirecting Anger for as long as you can remember and now you are changing to minor league Outrageousness (or some other minor leaguer). *Whatever you're switching to will feel strange at first.* It's supposed to! The strangeness is designed to make you aware of how you behave. The awkwardness is designed to help you begin conscious changes toward less and less destructive behavior habits until finally you are able to eliminate self-destructiveness from your life.

In order to help you give yourself permission to utilize negative behavior as a counteracting agent, consider the minor league forms of self-destructiveness as your "Safety Valves."

Safety Valves are concrete suggestions which are designed to be opened up when you are ready to blow up if you don't let off some pressure. Going on the assumption that you cannot stop doing your major self-destructive acts all at once, Safety Valves will allow you to slow down the destruction and begin to break the grip of the habit of self-destructive behavior.

A habit (and remember that self-destructiveness, major or minor, IS A HABIT) cannot always be dispelled by the mere determination to get rid of it; would this were the case. My idea is to break the ingrained response (it's easier to break it with an intermediate negative first) and then clear the track for the establishment of a new habit of positive, self-constructive behavior.

Safety Valves also serve a second function, perhaps even more important than the easing of pressure. In reading through them you will find a number of powerful negative suggestions, some of which will strike you as horrifying. This is exactly what I intended! These suggestions are designed to shock you. Call it a form of fantasy if you wish, but the purpose of the shock is to get you to break out of old, set patterns that you take for granted as being unbreakable.

Many of the conventions we live by have an extremely destructive side. By suggesting such *un*conventional behavior, I hope to help you crack the mold of the old habits and rethink some of your attitudes. Remember, the method I am using is my form of shock treatment!

Shock Therapy does exactly this—it jolts you out of the set place you're in and breaks the circuit you haven't been able to break by any other means. Another way (less ominous to most people) of describing shock therapy is "therapeutic brain stimulation." As such it provides the change you need to put your emotional set on a different plane. Electroconvulsive therapy (ECT) *as it is administered today* has proved to be immensely beneficial in the treatment of depressives for whom nothing else has worked and who are in a life-threatening condition from the risk of suicide or malnutrition as a result of loss of appetite.

No one is sure *exactly* how shock therapy works, but

123

they know that it does work in a great many cases. Suppose, then, that you try a different kind of shock based on the idea that "therapeutic brain stimulation" can be achieved by natural means as well as alien means. Suppose you use the innate power of your own thoughts to create the stimulation. What I am suggesting is that you live through the shock treatments that I will offer *in your imagination* with as much genuinely experienced reality as you can manage. Those things on the list which you can actually do without either damaging or embarrassing yourself should be done in actuality. Those things which are too strong or horrifying to do in actuality should be lived through in your mind *as if you were doing them in actuality*.

Try it. You will gain some new perspectives on yourself, your values, and the world you live in. Shock treatments are an extreme measure, so it might be well to discuss them beforehand with the people you live with if you do not live alone. In fact, your family or cohabitors should be let in on all the nostrums you use and the reasons you are using them. Their understanding can be helpful and may even increase the effectiveness. Who knows—they may decide to join you!

It cannot be overlooked that your cohabitors may be causing a lot of your depressions. Or at least it may feel that way. I think you should, in this case, let it be known that you are beginning to take steps to help yourself overcome your depression and that you would welcome all the constructive help and support and encouragement that might come your way. I think you must impart this information without apology or pleading, and without promises. *This is something you are doing for you!* Your spouse, parent, child, or other cohabitor can take as much or as little interest as he, she, or it wishes. If the time comes when you begin to uncover the deeper reasons for your depressions—and how they reach over and into the lives of those around you, which inevitably they will—then you will arrive at some decisions *together* about how to tackle the problems you share. But, for the moment, if taking on the problems of inter-relationships is too much, try for understanding and a cease-fire until you have time to gain some ground in your own struggle. Tackle yourself first. Save your familial network problems until you have some self-confidence, or get some outside specialized professional help.

The replacement of the minor leaguers is somewhat like using saccharin to replace sugar—they have their drawbacks, but they're a step in the right direction.

The effect of the "shock" should be to interrupt the habits of self-destructive behavior patterns—unwilling behavior patterns that are ingrained and insidious.

One thing I promise you—it will be interesting!

Safety Valves and Shock Treatments

If You Have Transferred To:	Try This:
Asociality	Don't answer your phone for a few days. Don't see anyone if you can help it. Don't go out. Stay at home, read, think, cry, pace, chew your nails. By Monday you'll be ready for contact with the world again.
Audacity	Send a telegram to your boss outlining all the reasons why you should be given a promotion or a raise. Ask for an RSVP. Send a telegram to someone you want to see socially—romantic interest or otherwise—and say you will call in a few days to make a date. Take a flyer on the market. Approach a stranger whose looks you like or whose clothes you admire and tell him or her.
Outrageousness	Devise a costume or outfit for yourself that is the diametric opposite of your usual image and wear it to a party

125

(Outrageousness)	(do not explain why you are doing it). Shout "Bravo" at the top of your lungs at the next play, concert or movie you attend that you really enjoy. Make a reservation at a fancy restaurant using a phony title—Baroness Mille-fiori or Count Sitzstuhl—dress and act the part. Buy some chewing tobacco and chew and spit in public. Try to convince a good friend or relative that you have decided to become a hustler.
Freakishness and Bizarre Entertainments	Spend an entire evening at home with your eyes bound; do not open them no matter what. Buy a pair of crutches; bind one or both legs and hobble around for two days. Cut off all your hair à la Yul Brynner. Go over Niagara Falls in a barrel. Scale a sky-scraper from the outside. Go hang-gliding. Learn to stunt-ride a motorcycle. Parachute out of an airplane. Buy one of the "blue" newspapers or magazines and read the classifieds. Answer one or two.
Self-Preoccupation	Go to an expensive beauty salon and have yourself "done" from head to toe (if you're male, so much the better). Join a health club that designs a program to suit your particular needs and

If You Have Transferred To:	Try This:
(Self-Preoccupation)	condition. Write your auto-biography. Insist on telling everyone you meet every detail of all of the above.
Carelessness and Indifference	Don't bathe for a week. Don't shave if it shows. Don't clean your apartment or house. Don't wash the dishes or put out the garbage. Don't throw out the newspapers for a month. Don't empty the cat's litter pan. Don't change the sheets or make the bed for a month. Don't go out of the house for a week. Don't eat regularly. Disregard any thought of good nutrition. Don't pick up your mail. Don't brush your teeth. If anyone speaks to you, look blank and walk away.
Avoidance	Don't look in the mirror. If anyone asks how you are, change the subject. If someone does something to hurt or upset you, ignore it and act as if nothing happened—in fact, act twice as nice to them. If you are short-changed, handle it by never going back there again. If you have lent something to someone which you now need, buy yourself a new one. Don't let anyone touch you. Don't touch anyone. Try your best not to touch yourself.

It is essential that the Minor league self-destructive clubs you choose are not ones you are already indulging in—otherwise the shock value would be lost.

As you do them—recall to yourself the major leaguers you have transferred from and try to make a connection with how shocking they would seem to you if they were not your habitual patterns of behavior.

Use the new perspectives you gain to reexamine what you do and why you do it.

As I have said earlier, this set of nostrums is intended to be forcefully negative and to work by contrast and opposites. Later chapters will offer the next progression to substitutions and replacements by positive, constructive nostrums.

CHAPTER 9

Stimulants Against Paralysis or Don't Just Lie There—Screw It!

Inevitably, one of the worst side effects of habitual depression is that it leads to a sense of futility. Futility is the prime cause of paralysis.

Paralysis, like everything else, affects you in different degrees and strikes different areas of your functional equipment. You may still be able to brush your teeth, but rubber tipping has become difficult and flossing is out of the question.

When you're lying there feeling paralyzed, you feel totally paralyzed. But you're not. Nevertheless, you have to deal with the fact that you *feel* you are. (That's the way you keep yourself flat out—by thinking that everything is impossible). Everything *is* impossible—if you try to take it all at once!

You won't want to, but begin by asking yourself to do the tiniest, most petite, smallest little thing you can imagine. Spend the first few minutes deciding what the smallest thing imaginable *is*. After you've done that, you will find that deciding was the smallest thing you could imagine— and that means you have already accomplished the first thing. You've started doing something.

You have given yourself the first little stimulant on the road to getting up off your back. In contrast to the kind of stimulation discussed in connection with entertainment depressions, stimulants against paralysis are targeted to evoke specific positive reactions rather than to replace the negative effects of boredom or the lack of sufficient interests.

Next, think about all the practical, ugly, unappetizing chores that you can't do, that you hate to even think about: the letters you have to write; the bills you must pay; the report you should make. Pick one of them and then make your next move—sharpen your pencil or take out your pen. The third thing you will accomplish is to actually write *one* check, or *one* sentence, or address *one* envelope. Just one. Do not attempt anything more at this point. Ask yourself for only the minimal gesture—a token, anything. And when you have done that one thing—*you must allow yourself to feel pleased and satisfied with the effort you have succeeded in making.* Don't underestimate how big or how important an accomplishment you have made!

The best method (perhaps the only method) for dealing with a mountain of paralysis is to take one small bite out of it. The first small bite will lead to another. The way over the mountain is to reduce it one bite at a time to a size you can manage. As long as you lie at the foot of it staring up, it will be impossible to scale. By standing up and taking one step, you reduce it to the possible.

By making only the tiniest demands on yourself, you are able to fulfill them. Fulfilling any demand puts positive feedback into your system and replaces the steady diet of negative feedback you've been getting from setting goals that are too difficult or too complex for an all-at-once thrust. It's not the goal, or the task, or the chore itself that paralyzes you—it's the negative feedback!

Piecemeal is one of the nicest words I know. I think of it as meaning "little bites"—little pieces of a meal.

Have you ever thought what would happen if you tried to eat a five-pound roast beef in one chunk? Not only would you choke to death, but you wouldn't enjoy the flavor. And you wouldn't have the pleasure of cutting it up and feasting on it bite by delicious bite—savoring each delectable morsel. (*Morsel* is another nice word.) Even the number of morsels is limited at one sitting—you would not gorge on the entire five-pound roast beef at one time by yourself. And the same thing applies when you feel like you've got a five-pound chunk of chore on your chest.

Taking the piecemeal approach, make yourself a modest list of morsels you might like to accomplish in one day. Actually write your list down and cross off each item after you've done it This is essential!

It might go like this:

1. Sit up.
2. Wash my face and comb my hair.
3. Rest.
4. Fix myself something to drink; coffee, tea, milk, juice.
5. Rest.
6. Get dressed.
7. Turn the radio or TV on.
8. Rest.
9. Get the mail.
10. Rest.
11. Telephone someone.
12. Turn off the radio or TV and rest.
13. Go to the grocery store and buy something to eat for dinner.
14. Rest.
15. Fix dinner and eat.
16. Rest.
17. Turn on the radio or TV.
18. Get undressed.
19. Turn off the radio or TV and go to bed.

If you can do six of the above items in one day, you'll have a leg over the saddle. I *guarantee* that there is no one who cannot do at least six. The secret is to think of each one as an accomplishment, no matter which ones you do, and the entire day's activity as an achievement—which indeed it will be!

Each thing you do which you recognize as an accomplishment will break the circuit of negative input. *What* you do is not as important as getting back into the pattern of doing. *The habit of thinking that you can do things is what is important.* Every time you congratulate yourself for an accomplishment, you reinforce your ability to accomplish something.

As you regain your confidence, your lists can become more sophisticated and you can ask more of yourself when you feel ready. No matter how much you ask of yourself, be sure to keep your items bite-size and tackle your goals in a step-by-step fashion, rewarding yourself and congratulating yourself *each* step of the way. Don't put down this one-step approach, thinking it's too simple or you're grown-up. Don't knock it or yourself for having to do it. Everybody who gets things done gets them done one at a time. When you see how well this works (whether or not you're depressed, this is the only way to achieve any goal), you'll be so pleased you'll tell everyone you know to "try it—you'll like it!"

There are five general kinds of nostrums to help you get moving when you feel paralyzed. Each one is assigned to a specific degree of paralysis, beginning with the mildest form and continuing in ascending order according to the amount of stimulus needed. They are: *competitiveness, fantasy, hope, anger,* and *illusion.* Read through them all and then try which ever one seems scaled to the degree of paralysis you feel at the moment. Different ones may work better for you at different times, so pick and choose.

Competitiveness

By its very nature, this stimulant cannot be taken when you are far gone This one is for a relatively light seizure— when you're balking, or just sitting there staring into space and wondering how to get going. You really don't feel like doing whatever it is you should be doing. It's like having a bit of cork stuck in the neck of your bottle. Your flow is seriously impeded. Competitiveness can serve as a sharp tap or two on the bottom to help dislodge the blockage and get your juices flowing again.

Take a look at the competition. What are they doing that you can't do? How far ahead of you are they? Are you willing to concede an inch, just because you don't "feel like it"?

A friend of mine, who recently started going to Weight Watchers, was having a very tough time following the strict regimen of weighing everything and writing every mouthful down. She went to a meeting and heard an eight-year-old boy report his very favorable progress for the week before. Her competitive spirit flared and she set her jaw—"If an eight-year-old can do it, I can!"

The difference between you and the competition is the one inch that you concede. Here is where the practice of sheer will power can help you learn self-discipline—and it is a learned skill, make no mistake about that.

One of the reasons I believe in a daily regimen (exercise is one, weighing food and writing every bite down is another) is that the repetition element, the "practice" of consistency, is a process of building. Undertaken sporadically, it is of no use whatsoever. Each day you must repeat your exercise or you lose the benefit of all the preceding days. (I am not speaking in an absolute sense—it is possible to skip a day or go off your regimen once in a while without losing everything, just as you can even stop for a longer period and not have to go back to the very beginning.) But as you add each day's regimen, you increase what you have at stake. So many pounds lost, so much muscle tone gained, so much self-discipline established. You will find that merely maintaining your discipline and noting your achievements will be highly motivating. The longer you continue it, the more there is at stake. If you stop smoking for a week, you don't want to lose that week . . . or month . . . or year.

So you ask yourself to have the discipline not to concede that inch today—either to your competitor or to yourself.

Competing with yourself is more challenging than competing with anyone else. It is also far more realistic and far more rewarding. Self-competition is a form of self-testing —of evaluating yourself. Who can resist one of those lists which asks you to "find out how well you score on the following?"

When you begin any endeavor, you have a certain entry-level ability, or endurance, or aptitude. That entry level becomes the mark you have to improve on. It is your landmark for gauging the effects of your practice, your guide to your rate of improvement and the measure of your increasing ability. As you work to lift yourself above that level, you are competing with yourself. You know when you can ask just a little bit more of yourself *and get it*. By asking it, and coming through for yourself, you stretch your capacity even further.

About a year ago, I decided to try to get myself into better physical condition. I had been sedentary for years and hated exercise. One of the exercises I undertook was an unsupported sitting position against a wall with my thighs parallel to the ground, and my feet planted firmly together on the floor. It was excruciatingly difficult. To maintain this position for fifteen seconds was almost more than I could stand. Day in and day out I went through this and gradually increased to twenty seconds, thirty seconds, forty-five seconds, and so on. At each new level, I had a sense of accomplishment and the knowledge that I would have more to lose if I stopped.

I worked my way up to the point where I could maintain this position for three full minutes. But when I went on vacation for five weeks, with all the sightseeing and walking, I let my exercises go. When I returned home, I could not do any of my exercises for the length of time I had achieved before I left. But within two weeks, I had already reached two and a half minutes on the "wall sitting" position and had regained my stamina completely on all the others.

Even if you stop for a while, regaining your place is easier than attaining it (if you don't let it go too long). On days when I feel lazy, I remind myself that I have done my exercises before, that I can do as many today as I did yesterday—and if I choose, I can even do more. I am, in effect, using my *self* as a stimulant in competition.

Knowing what you could or should be doing—and aren't—can give you enough "pop" to blow the cork out of your way. Competitiveness is stimulating. When you need a little extra drive, take one or two good snorts after resting.

Fantasy

Fantasy is a form of home movies which *you* write, direct, produce, and act in. You can create certain flicks to project on your inner screen—flicks for pure enjoyment or distraction, for edification (as when you want to replay a scene to study your moves or try out new ones), and particularly fantasy flicks for stimulation when they are linked to hope.

You may be feeling down because you have already done everything you can toward the accomplishment of a certain goal and have not yet had any results. You then feel somewhat paralyzed because, while there are other things to do (and other goals), you don't really feel like making new efforts. This kind of downer is connected to what I call payoff lag, and it can be a long, drawn-out period.

To get you up and going, making inroads on new and different goals, I suggest fantasy flicks featuring stories about how it will be when the longed-for payoff does come. How will it affect your life? How will it change you? What new goals will it lead to?

Fantasy movies will enable you to consider some of the real factors you may have to deal with as a result of this coming life-change. Like living through and trying out experiences in your imagination when you are budging your boulders or when you are transferring your majors to the minors, you can evaluate a new condition or possibility calmly—*if you are not in the middle of the actual change itself*. In this way, fantasy brings you pleasure, and a forward-looking, positive frame of mind. It lets you plot and ploy to your heart's content and accomplish practical gains at the same time.

When you are partially paralyzed and half-inclined to feel that you will never realize your heart's desire, take matters into your own head and realize your goal come true in fantasy. You have paid the price of admission by doing the work ahead of time. You don't have to wait for your payoff to come to you. You can go out to meet it and taste the joy of fulfillment when you choose.

Fantasy can be a healthy, pleasurable, constructive opiate which will relieve your blues and strengthen your confidence in yourself. Once you release your imagination, the ways you can use it to help yourself are almost limitless.

Take this stimulant when the occasion warrants. Take a deep drag, inhale—and dream!

Hope

The next step of paralysis may occur when the payoff lag goes on for an inordinate length of time: It continues past any reasonable period and despair of change sets in. You feel that you will never get past the impasse, that you have gotten to the point where you think yourself a fool for ever having thought you could do anything.

You've heard all the axioms about "something's got to give," or "something's bound to happen," but when you're lying there staring up at the ceiling counting the cracks and the phone doesn't ring, and the mail only brings bills and nothing you were counting on is coming through—then this moment is forever. You're suspended in limbo; you feel painted into a landscape of futile waiting, immobilized in time and space. I remember once when everything in my life was so bleak for such a protracted period of time that I began to feel that I simply wanted to lie without moving until my body rotted.

Anyone who has suffered from payoff lag can identify with the lost-on-a-deserted-island story. You keep putting your messages in bottles and sending them out into the limitless sea. And it feels like there will never be anyone out there to pick up your message and respond to your call. Robinson Crusoe did the best possible thing by making a worthwhile (not to say fascinating) life for himself while he was waiting to be found. In fact, he did so well that many would prefer the life he created for himself to the one he longed to rejoin. Still, while he was creating his special deserted-island life, he was hoping for a change. Whether or not he had second thoughts *after* the change came is meat for discussion.

136

Ordinarily, hope is a thing we all have naturally and easily. But frustration can defeat hope and bring about a situation in which you punish yourself for ever having hoped before by not allowing yourself to hope again. This kind of punishment, like a form of superstition, is based on an irrational idea that by not hoping, you will not jinx yourself. By not hoping, you will have a better chance of getting the thing you are hoping for.

Hope is a very tricky commodity. You can't live without it, but too much can make you sick—especially on an empty stomach!

There is a proverb in the Old Testament which says:

Hope deferred maketh the heart sick.
But desire fulfilled is a tree of life.

As is the case with all proverbs or other pieces of wisdom, they are wise because you interpret them to suit your own situation. You shape and hone the meaning to fit you. In the proverb quoted above, the interpretation rests on a question of timing. But timing is a highly individual reaction. Some people might make a good case for deferred fulfillment, arguing that waiting for a reward makes it sweeter when you get it. And in many instances, it does: "you only appreciate what you have to work hard to get . . ." "easy come, easy go . . ."

My experience is that desire fulfilled is sweetest when it comes after the hardest work, with perhaps just a little delay thrown in to allow anticipation to sharpen your satisfaction.

Hope must be grounded in effort: either effort already made; effort planned; or effort in the making. Preferably all three.

When you are partially paralyzed, you must allow yourself to acknowledge unrealized goals and hope for their fulfillment. You must not punish yourself by withdrawing your hope—even though you believe you are doing what may be considered the equivalent of crossing your fingers against evil tidings by denying hope.

Use hope—that is what it is intended for.
Use hope to make new efforts.

Use hope to take new directions.

Hope and work pulling together as a team make a happy charioteer.

When you use hope as a stimulant, *sip it between bites of hard work*.

Anger

Anger impels! And, as I discussed in chapter five, you can use it to gather up your emotions and shape them into a hard fist. Anger can be the driving force, the energy that galvanizes you into action. When you get angry, you don't sit still and bemoan your miserable fate. When you get angry, you jump up and kick something or curse something—both of which are forms of release. Release means to let out—not to hold in where it eats your liver. The image of Prometheus * having his liver gnawed daily by a vulture because he stole fire from heaven as a gft for us mortals is, to my mind, one of those examples from Jungian depth psychology: a "myth" that is not a chance story or a meaningless bit of symbolism. It expresses, through symbols, a universal truth about mankind, the meaning of which is grasped by all indviduals in the deepest part of their unconscious minds. For in Jungian psychology, each individual carries the entire history of the human species within him/herself and is connected to all other members of the human species, past, present, and future through means of the representation of "types"—in Jungian terms, "archetypes." Prometheus is an archetype

* According to ancient Greek mythology, Prometheus was one of the race of giants (Titans) who lived on earth before the creation of man. To him and his brother Epimetheus, Zeus gave the task of creating man and all the other animals. When Prometheus looked down from Mount Olympus and saw that the beasts were devouring man, his creation, he asked Zeus to allow him to give man fire for heat and light and protection. Zeus refused, but Prometheus stole fire from the sun and gave it to man anyway. His punishment was to be chained to a mountain peak where a vulture would come each day and devour his liver. Each night it would grow back again. Finally Hercules climbed the peak and freed Prometheus.

who represents the hero theme. To take it one step further, it seems to me that the "vulture" in the Prometheus myth is a symbol for anger held in or repressed—that's why it's gnawing on his liver. Anger *is* fire, symbolically speaking, and when used properly and directed, like fire, it is a gift.

As children, we learn to fear the expression of anger (as we learn not to play with matches or hot stoves or boiling water) because it can be dangerous. When adults—who are so big and powerful and threatening—exhibit anger, we are afraid because of what they might do to us. Many adults fear God's wrath in exactly the same way. By comparison, they feel small and helpless and vulnerable —like children.

So called irrational fears—whether they are fears of anger, height, water, criticism, or anything else—all carry the element of threat. Threat is rational. Even when the threat is more imagined than real, the fear is real.

Uncontrolled anger is not just a threat. Uncontrolled anger is a frightening and dangerous element. Blind rage can be lethal. But I am not advocating rage. I am not advocating anything blind or savage. To the contrary, I am advocating the use of righteous indignation, justified irritation, and understandable impatience. Most of all I am advocating that the feelings *behind* anger be mobilized, organized, and directed toward a meaningful goal . . . *under control.*

Not long ago, a recently widowed woman I know was suffering from a bad depression. Not only had she lost her mate, but every day she discovered different things she couldn't do, different areas of living she had simply left to her husband to take care of, different ways she now felt inadequate. She felt resentment and also a sense of having been babied too much; but all in all, she felt overwhelmed by having to cope with everything herself.

The predicament came to a head when she decided to have a little home decorating done to cheer herself up. First on her list was getting someone to re-tile the kitchen floor. Two weeks later, after several delays and broken appointments, she was more depressed than ever—she felt that now she couldn't even manage a simple problem like getting some work done for herself. She wallowed in feeling sorry for herself for a while. But then she got blisteringly angry about being *dependent*. She got so angry that she didn't care how much of a mess she made—she was going to lay the tiles herself. It couldn't be *that* hard.

She got a do-it-yourself home-repair book and studied the section on flooring. Timorously, she began the work. She made a few mistakes in the beginning, but none were unrectifiable. And within a short time, she had mastered the art of laying linoleum floor tiles.

She made a fine job of it, and when she had finished, she felt a sense of accomplishment and pride that she hadn't felt in months. She was so pleased with the job and with herself that she decided to study other sections of the book and try other projects.

When last contacted, she was happily fixing up her home and enjoying a newfound sense of competency and accomplishment. There's no telling where she will go from here, but she will go somewhere. This woman used her anger to blast herself into an entirely new place.

It is only the fear of uncontrolled anger—uncontrolled violence—that causes people to repress all feelings vaguely resembling those that they fear. The feelings themselves cannot be stifled. They can only be held in where they gnaw your liver. Tap them! Harness them! Use them to work for you against the obstacles you want to overcome and toward the goals you want to achieve.

Anger as a stimulant should be taken as a shot in the arm.

Illusion

Different from fantasy, illusion is a way of dealing with reality which you use in practical, everyday life without thinking about it. You live with illusions: that the earth will endure forever, that the sun will inevitably rise and set, that you will get up in the morning and lie down at night, that you will never die. In an immediate sense, these are not illusions, for they enable you to function on a day-to-day basis. I call them functioning illusions, and the person who is suffering from a really deep depression needs them more than anyone else.

140

When you are truly depressed, the hardest thing in the world is to believe that what you do in life matters; that who you are matters; that your acts make a difference to someone; that you can better your existence; that caring and trying, wanting and desiring are worthwhile emotions; and that you have love to give and gifts to share. All these things may seem like illusions to you when you are down. Let them be. Let them be "functioning illusions" for you, because without them it would not be worthwhile for anybody to get up out of bed in the morning. Why bother?

Until you have the faith to believe in these things, accept them if you must as functioning illusions, for they will enable you to affirm life, not deny it. Without the belief that you matter, you cannot aim for tomorrow. You cannot work and plan and dream of attaining your goal unless you have some notion that it could possibly come true. Choosing to believe in possibilities is as practical as choosing to believe in the sunset. Look around you and you will see all the dreams humankind has made come true.

Yes, there are plenty of defeated dreams lying around out there—but the only sure way to defeat a dream is not to attempt to fulfill it!

Goals are essential to every human being. Small, medium, large, grandiose—everybody has to aim for something. Having a goal is the best reason in the world for getting up in the morning.

It is my absolute conviction that your choices dictate how your life seems to you—meaningless or worthwhile, full or empty, sweet, bitter, sour, tangy—much of it is your choice, because *all of it can be valuable if you choose to view the experience of tasting with curiosity and relish.*

It may be that dire things will befall our planet or our solar system in millions of years. It may be that dire things will befall you tomorrow. But if you live your whole life worrying about dire things befalling all over the place, you'll never be able to move a muscle. Guaranteed.

Nobody knows for sure about tomorrow or a million years from now. I am writing that very quietly—nobody knows for sure. Meanwhile, what you do know for sure is that lying there on your back contemplating perfect futility for the entire universe (and yourself along with it) is destruction here and now.

DOLDRUMS CHART

Degree of Paralysis and Symptoms	Area Affected
1st: Laziness; mild ennui; tired of your own complaints; usual interests seem flat; no zest; resolve is there but no ignition.	Downhearted
2nd: Listlessness; restiveness; fatigue; loss of appetite; loss of ability to concentrate.	Softheaded
3rd: Body refuses to get up off the chair; sleep all the time or not at all; no interest in sex; head tilted downward.	Weak-kneed
4th: All bodily extremities are limp; inability to make any decisions; movements feel uncoordinated.	Lame-brained
5th: No wish to move even an eyelid; feel like you are in a state of hibernation; body feels like it weighs four hundred tons naked.	Everything

General Kind of Nostrum	Specific Nostrums
Competitiveness	Invite three friends for bridge; go bowling with someone; work the crossword puzzle with your lover; see how long you can hold your breath; begin a routine of daily exercises which increase as you go along; learn speed reading.
Fantasy	Select your most hoped for turn of events and run an entire movie of it in your head; project the possible problems and solutions; imagine how every area of your life will be affected; *think it has actually happened*.
Hope	Write down all possibilities of success on one side of a sheet of paper and all possibilities of failure on another. Compare them. Tear up the failure sheet. Believe in what's left!
Anger	Punch a punching bag; curse like a sailor; dredge up every four-letter word you ever heard and repeat them at increasing decibel levels periodically, slowly adding the names of persons on whom you would like to vent your spleen; throw whatever loose pillows you have across the room, follow them, and kick them back to the other side; break a piece of glass or pottery by putting it in a bag and smashing it or stomping on it.
Illusion	Think about the history of our planet and place yourself in perspective against that thought; consider that your brain is capable of

(Illusion)   fitting the whole shebang in all its
                      grandeur in there. Place your mo-
                      ment of paralysis in the perspective
                      of your whole life and the entire
                      history of the universe. Think about
                      better things to think about.

So, let us opt for huge doses of illusions—swallow whole
as needed. Believe that everything matters, baby, because
by so believing, you make everything matter!

As a handy guide out of the doldrums, the chart on
pages 142–144 shows which general and which specific
nostrums to apply for each degree of paralysis.

If *none* of the nostrums on the Doldrums Chart works
for you, there are two more things you can try:

First—accept the fact that there is nothing you can do
at the moment, so you'll just have to wait it out. **Tread
water till the tide changes.**

Second—if you can't stand to wait it out and you really
do want to end it all . . . okay. Decide that you will do it.
But before you can carry it out, *you must do the following:*
make a list of everything you have ever wanted to do in
life but have not done because you were too "nice," too
broke, too scared, too timid, too finicky, too bourgeois, or
too tied up in knots. Next, starting at the top of the list,
do at least *three* things on the list before you kill yourself.

I absolutely guarantee that this will get you out of your
depression if nothing else does! But before you get to this
"in extremis" condition, do me a favor, will you? **Think
about *why* this last nostrum will work and apply the principle to your everyday living.**

CHAPTER 10

When and How to Give in to It
or
How to Be a Rebel with a Cause

One of the scourges of modern life which we inherited from Queen Victoria is the "stiff upper lip"—the step-brother of the "work ethic." This expression originated when some shrewd observer noticed that when you are fighting like crazy against all your natural impulses, you grind your teeth. It is almost impossible to grind your teeth without stiffening your upper lip. Therefore, the origins of the saying are purely descriptive. Go to the mirror, grind your teeth, and see for yourself. I'm not saying that you can't keep a stiff upper lip without grinding your teeth, or that you can't grind your teeth without keeping a stiff upper lip—you probably can if you try hard enough. The two just seem to go together, that's all.

As is the case with most things that we embrace and choke to death in an overzealously loving grasp, there is something good to be derived from the stiff-upper-lip syndrome—but the trouble comes in when it's made into an ethic. The *good* in work does not lie in an ethic, either. However, I guess we always go around making immutable laws out of good ideas so we won't forget them. This is how the ancient Jews developed the idea of *kosher* into a law. *Kosher* means "clean," and the best way to prevent certain numbskulls from eating contaminated food was to make it a law. This way, folks could simply obey without thinking. As you know, I opt for thinking every time—but then, the seeds of anarchy are buried in this soil, so watch out! Not eating pork that had been hanging around out in the sun for too long and was making for a lot of trichinosis, ptomaine or other poisons was a practical necessity. Then. Now the whole matter has become cultural, and that's an entirely different story.

Getting back to what all this has to do with fighting depression—there is a connection with the stiff upper lip. That's cultural, too. Many times it may be good for you to keep one—but sometimes you can't fight the blues (particularly the habitual blues) by wrestling them to the ground. No matter how many fancy holds you try, there are times when you need to give in gracefully and let your shoulders be pinned.

Choose When and Choose How

What counts is that *you* decide to give in. You choose when and you choose how. In other words, *even when giving in, you keep control.*

This is the same principle you use when you are training your pet—there are moments when you must relent (even the dentist pauses in drilling now and then to give your nerves a rest). You must sense that it's time to give the little rascal a breather—your pet's nerves need to relax, too—and *you* give the breather. Under no circumstances can you allow your pet to break training because it decides it doesn't want to do its duty. You simply cannot leave this decision in your pet's paws. That's bad training (or *no* training), and leads to stains on your carpet or on your pillow every time your pet gets peeved.

In effect, I want you to become your own pet, with everything that entails—including the loving care and the training. So every now and then you have to give your nerves a rest by giving in to your depression.

The next thing to discuss is *how*.

A fine way to give in is to break training by *rebellion*. In chapter eight, I discussed a number of ways to substitute the minor forms of self-destructiveness for the major forms. Now we're ready to move up to substituting constructive ways of rebellion. I call this section Rebellion by Constructive Substitutes. It'll never make a song lyric, but there's meat on them bones. Constructive substitutes will include different ways of negotiating with yourself—*deals, bargains, reversals, and interspersions*—all of which are different sets of maneuvers for rebelling with a cause.

Deals

The *deal* involves choosing total immersion in the pits for a prescribed period of time. A *deal* you make with yourself is just like a *deal* you make with anyone else—it has got to be good for both parties. (Go ahead, split yourself up, it'll help with the distance you need, and a little schizoid behavior can be very enlightening if you know how to use it.)

"Honey baby," you might say to yourself, "have I got a deal for you!"

This will immediately gain your undivided attention, because you have never been able to resist your own deals.

Continuing, you add, "Here it is: you're feeling rotten, low, mean, and ugly and you hate even the thought of trying to improve matters, right?"

(Give yourself time to agree.)

"Right."

"You've already tried umpteen thousand things . . . all the nostrums in the book . . . and *nothing* has worked. So what's the point? Right?"

(This is the "Pond of Despond" routine, so you wait for agreement again.)

"Get to the point," you answer, becoming impatient.

"Okay—the deal is, *don't* try to do anything. Just lie there and soak it in for a while. Indulge yourself to the hilt. Wallow. Slosh. Crawl. Do the backstroke in it . . . for a set amount of time. The *deal* is: you can wallow away for say, the next three hours, or four, or sixteen—but you have to concentrate on your mud hole *and nothing else* the whole time! You have to slosh without distraction from the sloshing, crawl until you are sick to death of crawling, wallow until your hide is shriveled up from wallowing . . . until the predetermined time period is up. The cost of the *deal* is to stick it out in the slough for the agreed-upon length of time, regardless of whether or not you continue to want to.

This is a very tricky *deal* to pull on yourself. If you think it isn't, try it! I won't tell you what will happen in the middle of your wallow, but you must stick with your *deal* once you enter it! I will offer you one small bit of advice—*don't set your wallow time for too long a period.* Protracted wallowing is harder than you think.

Compromises

The *compromise* is the maneuver that lets you do something that is good for you even though it may not be the thing you need most urgently at the time. This approach shares some similarities with the negotiations you undertake with your inner demons (your "ID") back in chapter two. It involves give and take, back-and-forth exchanges of needs—and finally, a settlement. Again, the "talks" are between you and you, and they might go something like this:

YOU #1: I know I should rewrite my résumé but I don't feel like it.

YOU #2: Do you want a job or do you not want a job?

YOU #1: That's a stupid question. I've rewritten the damned résumé sixteen times and what good does it do?

YOU #2: Complain, complain, complain—that's all you ever do. No wonder nobody wants to hire you.

YOU #1: That's not very helpful; you don't have to put me down.

YOU #2: You're right. If you don't feel like rewriting your résumé, what do you feel like doing?

YOU #1: Nothing. I just want to lie here forever.

YOU #2: Sorry, pal, I can't go along with that—we have an interview tomorrow morning and we have to get ready. I want us to be sharp as a whistle.

YOU #1: Tack. The expression is "sharp as a tack."

YOU #2: Whatever . . . but I want to go to that interview tomorrow ready, willing, and able.

YOU #1: Why don't you come up with something constructive for a change?

YOU #2: Tell you what—let's *compromise*. Put the résumé aside. But get up and wash your hair, iron your clothes and get ready. We'll go to the interview tomorrow and do our best. If we don't get the job, we'll ask them what qualifications we lack. Maybe we'll learn something useful that will help us with the résumé later. After we get ready, we can go to a movie.

YOU #1: You got it!

Bargains

The *bargain* is slightly different from either the *deal* or the *compromise* negotiation. The *bargain* involves indulging yourself in pure distraction, either before or after you do something good for yourself.

The *bargain* is, of course, built on the reward system—you are, in effect, rewarding yourself for doing something that will benefit you by giving yourself a distraction, a goof-off. Again, the principle is to take matters into your own hands. Rather than sit around waiting or hoping for or expecting a reward from outside because you've been good, *you give yourself the reward*. This way you are sure of getting it, because you are not depending on someone else to give it to you.

When you've had a string of disappointments in the rewards department and your ensuing depression is circumstantial (but in danger of becoming habitual because of the length of the string), *you need a guarantee*. If you're already in a habitual depression, you need a guarantee even more.

149

This is the time for you to make the *bargain*. And, if you wish, you can collect your reward before you give out.

Okay, dearie," you say to yourself "here's the *bargain:* if you lose five pounds, I'll buy you the best seats in the house to whatever show you want to see. *You* can take *Charlie* for a change."

Sometimes it is important to feel that *you* can be the one to do the shortchanging if you want, rather than be the one who gets shortchanged. Even when you are making the *bargain* with yourself and the one who would get cheated is also yourself, it is important to feel that you have the control. If you decide that you want to collect the reward and not do something that is good for you, you can't! I doubt seriously that you will ever be tempted to cheat or shortchange yourself, but it's important that you will be getting your goodies out front for a change, and you will be in control of issuing or withholding your own rewards.

I remember once, when I was a child, two of my boyfriends from the neighborhood suggested that they would show me theirs if I would show them mine. I agreed and, naively, went first. You will not be too surprised to hear that immediately after I had kept my end of the bargain, they both ran off. This was my first lesson in skepticism, but somehow I didn't really learn it. I kept on going first most of my life, and I can't tell you how many times I've put out without receiving the payoff. I am still trusting, and I wouldn't change that for the world. But when I am feeling depressed because things have not worked out the way I was promised, I need to feel that I can take matters into my own hands and, if necessary, collect first and show later.

In carrying out the *bargain,* as with *deals* and *compromises,* you must keep *both* ends—the doing-good part and the reward part.

It is essential that you stick to each of these maneuvers *to the letter,* because:

You have to be able to trust *you.*
You have to know that you *can* trust you.

Rebellion by Constructive Substitutes is a nostrum to use when you are feeling very balky about using the other nostrums—the things-that-are-good-for-you nostrums. There is a shadowy area, however. When you are feeling somewhat balky, but not stony balky, you may just require a little gentle manipulation. Manipulation by Constructive Substitutes is the name of this tactic, and it is carried out by *reversals* and *interspersions*.

Reversals

A *reversal* is absolutely simple and almost idiotically childish, but it works.

Let's say you have made yourself a lengthy list of chores to accomplish for the day. You have organized yourself down to the last minute and you know you can get it all done if you keep at it. Great. Go to it, tiger!

There's only one hitch: "Tiger" doesn't want to. Tiger doesn't feel like being organized. Tiger wants to lie abed all day eating chocolates and reading dirty books.

You prod Tiger three, four, five times, and all Tiger does is lie there emitting surly growls.

What to do?

Frankly, it isn't rebellion Tiger really wants, it's the *idea* of rebellion. That's understandable; after all, Tiger is only human. All you have to do is "handle" Tiger—humor Tiger a little bit and you'll have a pussycat again. A sure way to turn the growls into purrs is to tear up the list and let Tiger do everything in reverse order, or mixed order, or random order, or out of order . . . or any order so long as it is not the order on the original list.

Tiger gets a wonderful sense of rebelling (at least against the order) and a sense of getting away with something because you tore up the list—so Tiger does everything on the list anyway, but has experienced the feeling of freedom of choice while doing it.

You can even use a reverse maneuver by telling Tiger *not* to do a certain item on the list. A paradoxical admonition can be marvelously efficacious, and Tiger is sure to do that one thing if nothing else.

Not only does this work, but at the conclusion of it, you will feel smart and wonderful for having successfully manipulated Tiger and for having virtuously accomplished things on the list. Tiger will feel wonderful, too, for not having knuckled under, for having gotten away with something, and for having done all those good things for you . . . you and Tiger.

Interspersions

Interspersions are as idiotically and childishly simple as reversals, and they work just as well. You simply take Tiger's same list, but this time you alternate reward activities with chore activities. For example, it's Saturday and you have to do four things before lunch: iron clothes, do your exercises, go to the supermarket, and take Suzy to her dance class.

However, this morning the mail brought a letter turning you down on the part-time job you had been hoping to get. You'd had high hopes and had been waiting to hear for several weeks. Now those hopes are dashed.

Plunk—pit time.

Then you say, "To hell with the four things before lunch! In fact, to hell with lunch. To hell with everything!"

Next you utter the five magic questions:

"What's the use?"

"Who cares?"

"So what?"

"Why try?"

"Will it ever be otherwise?"

You're ready for the garbage heap.

Allow yourself to lie there for a while gently licking your morning's wound and bathing it in a light saline solution. Then, one of the first things to try is an *interspersion*.

You tell yourself, "Okay. Forget the four things before lunch—do *one* thing and then reward yourself. We'll see about the other three afterward."

So you iron the clothes.

Then, as a reward, you call up a sympathetic friend and talk about the miseries of being a housewife in a society where success is based on how much money you earn. Your friend, being in the same boat, commiserates nicely.

You feel a little better—so you do your exercises.

Now intersperse a lovely warm shower and wash your hair. Then, since you feel good about taking care of yourself, get in the car and go to the supermarket. Upon your return home after stowing the groceries, you make a cup of coffee and drink it while musing on the mortal condition.

Finally, philosophically primed for the outside world, you take Suzy to her class. You have accomplished everything you set out to do this morning and still catered to yourself while you were feeling down, so you feel good on both counts. You and Tiger will live and flourish to fight another day and win another battle. In fact, you're feeling so much better because you didn't let it beat you that you begin to plan a whole campaign for where else to apply for that job you want.

No matter what you're trying to motivate yourself to get up and do, *reversals* and *interspersions* work because they offer you the change that you need. *Deals, compromises,* and *bargains* work for the same reason. Whether you manipulate yourself or you rebel, you're releasing some of the pressure. You're giving in without giving in, which doubles your reasons for being pleased with yourself.

So, when none of the other nostrums works . . . give in. But give in by choice and by design. You keep your discipline going (remember, you are keeping the control by deciding to rebel) without feeling that you are rigidly compulsive. It's sort of a flexible straitjacket situation. You feel that you have rebelled, and yet you've accomplished what you had to do in the first place. You win both ways—and I'll play in that kind of game anytime!

Just remember, a little anarchy goes a long way.

CHAPTER 11

Shopping for Help

Suppose you have just entered a supermarket. You take one of the large shopping carts and, weekly list in hand, you set off down the aisle. There are a few basic categories on your list: meat, vegetables, fruit, dairy, baked goods, cleaning products—and a couple of goodies. There will be things to drink, some seasoning ingredients, maybe even a magazine.

Now within the basic categories, your choices are enormous. There are assorted brands to select from, different cuts of meat, types of animal or fish, kinds of fruit and vegetables, styles of preparation, forms of packaging, range of price, and quantity of item, to name a few.

Different approaches in therapy can be viewed in much the same way as the diverse commodities on the grocery store shelves. There are relatively few basic categories—but within each there's an enormous variation in terminology, approach, style, technique, aim, philosophy, focus, and slant. There are many, many ways of saying the same thing; many, many angles from which to view the same phenomenon. Some graffiti I saw on a fence summed it up nicely: "José got mental health." That's what we're all shopping for.

When you are emotionally upset, you do go shopping for help. List in hand, you start looking around for things to satisfy your needs. Depending on how careful or canny a shopper you are—or how given to impulse buying—you may read every word on each label; you may just automatically pick up the items you're used to (such as the telephone); you may consciously or unconsciously select because of price considerations (emotional or monetary). You may even eschew securing help because you feel it is a luxury item and too costly for your purse or your personality.

I urge you to be a careful, wise shopper. Pay attention to the wares you pick up and take home with you. Inform yourself as best you can concerning their nutritional value, the additives and preservatives, the purity, the price, and, of course, the appeal and suitability to your needs and condition.

Once you find standard items that work for you—that satisfy *your* criteria—stick with them. But don't be afraid to try something new once in a while. You may find something new that suits you better than your old familiar product. You change—and it may be necessary to change your means of therapy if you outgrow it or find a more beneficial solution.

We tend to want a perfect product—like manna—which will taste to each of us like the thing we love most, will fall on us from heaven, will be ideally balanced nutritionally, will require little or no preparation or work, will never fail to satisfy our taste buds, and will cost absolutely nothing. Because this is what we want, we fall prey to certain myths. Some of these myths are: cause and effect; universal answers; instant change; instant help; single, simple solutions; and the notion that contradictions are mutually exclusive.

Our myths revolve around one great hunger—the hunger for things to come easy. Human beings, the most fantastically, horrendously complex organisms, long for simplicity like desert sand longs for water. The funny part is that, the minute we are handed one of these simple solutions, we denigrate it by saying, "That's too simple."

The way I see it is this: the solutions to emotional (or psychological or mental or living) problems are both simple and complex at the same time. They are simple on the surface, fantastically complex on a deeper level, and simple once again at the very heart.

Depending on how I look at myself at a given moment,

I will see my problems in different lights, and I will try to apply different methods to them.

The simplicity at the surface is a different simplicity from the one at the heart—although often, in dealing with the problem in a practical sense, you will find that the differences are of no consequence. It is nice to know how something works and to understand the principle on which it rests, but it is not necessary. When I was twelve years old, I asked my older brother to teach me how to drive a car. "Okay," he agreed. He got a piece of paper and pencil and to my utter amazement started to draw the mechanics of how an automobile works, explaining the principle to me as he went along. When I complained, he said, "If you're going to drive a car, I want you to understand how one works."

Between you and me, he was a very clever guy, and while his lesson did not get me to understand the principle of the combustion engine, it did successfully forestall my entry onto the roads and highways of America until I was at least able to see over the windshield.

This story also illustrates the myth that contradictory facts must necessarily exclude each other. One or the other must be true, you often will say. I say *both* can be true *at the same time*. My brother was right in feeling that I should understand the principle of the automobile if I were going to drive one, but that did not exclude my being right in not wanting to get into all that before taking the wheel. The so-called Western mind has a lot of trouble with the ability to accept the validity—even the importance —of contradiction. Eastern minds do not have this problem, but to an American or a European, the notion is anathema; we are always thinking either/or. Like my friend who could not feel both attractive *and* smart, we tend not to believe that you can be both rich *and* selfless, loving *and* critical, generous *and* frugal, painstaking *and* flexible, discriminating *and* accepting, emotional *and* intellectual.

Children know you can want different things at the same time. When you ask a child (before it gets brainwashed in the "mutually exclusive" myth), "Which do you want, a ride on the merry-go-round or an ice cream cone?" The child will quite normally answer, "Both." He won't see

156

the need to choose between two things or ideas that both have something desirable to offer, and neither do I!

What is interesting is that we become conditioned to the idea of things being mutually contradictory and therefore mutually exclusive, and accept this without thinking about it. If somebody says to you, "What kind of psychotherapy do you think works the best, Freudian or Jungian or Adlerian?" you are set up to make an excluding choice. Automatically, your mind begins picking the "best" and rejecting the others out of hand.

Getting back to the supermarket. Suppose you have your list of needs in hand and you want to fill them all. Eating steak is not going to satisfy your need for fruit, and you certainly can't clean the bathroom tile with an apple, so why should you expect to satisfy all your emotional or psychological problem-needs with one item?

Some "mental health" needs are therapeutic (meaning, in this case, that they should be served by a professional therapist); some are educational (meaning, in this case, that they require new thinking or new learning); some are relational (meaning that they should be served by social or personal contact); and some, perhaps most, are individual (meaning that they represent the individual's needs to work out his or her own life—to understand him/herself and to come to terms with the meaning of his/her existence.

A shrink can't serve *all* of your needs. I don't care what cut of meat he or she may be! *You* have to take care of a lot of them, and you have to find as many ways of taking care of them as you possibly can. As I said early in the book, first you have to sort yourself out and *make distinctions* among your needs. Allocate them and seek what will serve them wherever you can find suitable answers.

Your needs are ongoing, and so must your provisioning be. You are shopping regularly for ideas, suggestions, techniques, approaches, and even gimmicks—the psychological equivalent of empty-caloried foods. There may be a time and place for junk food and there may be a time and place for gurus or cult figures. These would not be *my* choice, but you have to make your own.

Even reading this book is a way of shopping for ideas that may help you. The more the merrier, as long as you exercise your powers of discernment and discretion. In other words, be careful about what you pop into your insides.

Philosophy and religion are solid, well-established, and reliable sources of food for thought. Dip into them and squeeze out the precious drops of nourishment, or balm or wisdom, or ethics, or insights, or morality, or whatever you may glean that can add to your life. Before there was psychology or medicine or social science, there was religion and philosophy. The phraseology differs from field to field, but many of the underlying concepts are the same, and many more overlap. Everybody is walking around the same boulder and describing it from her or his own particular point of view. The boulder is, in one sense, the life you find yourself trying to live. You can gain insights from the diverse points of view from each discipline, which may help you sort out your own understanding of what it's all about.

You Don't Have To Choose Either/Or!

You can investigate est, primal screaming, bioenergetics, Rogerian therapy, Gestalt therapy, psychodrama, transactional analysis, behavioral-directive therapies, and many offshoots and bypaths of any of the above. There will be something for you in almost everything you examine— something that you can apply as a principle, an insight, or a signpost. Even if you are turned off by an approach, remember that somebody is turned on, so you can at least appreciate an approach and sometimes learn a great deal by discovering why it doesn't suit you.

There is an excellent book I can recommend which will give you a sampling of what's available nowadays in the field of psychotherapy. It's *A Complete Guide to Therapy: From Psychoanalysis to Behavior Modification,* by Dr. Joel Kovel (available in paperback from Pantheon Books). By the time you read through Kovel's book, I think you'll have done a lot of shopping and selecting and comparison. Be open; try what sounds feasible to you. It matters not what something is called, but whether it works! In the Appendix, I've given thumbnail sketches of the newer of these therapies. I hope they will stimulate you to find out more about how much there is to choose from.

Throughout the book I have discussed making distinctions and breaking things down into bite-size pieces. Now let me also mention the validity and value of the holistic approach to self-understanding. Therapy serves *you* as a whole entity. The benefits you derive from it cannot be neatly split between "therapy which prevents depression" and "therapy for coping with depression"—except for what is called "crisis intervention." By and large, therapy of any kind is being put into your larder, stored and stocked for use according to your need and as you see fit. It is there for you for coping *and* for preventing, for dealing with active onslaughts of depression and for meliorating the factors that cause them to develop.

When you consider which choices to make in selecting your staples, be open but discriminating, honest but appraising. Don't think that every mote of help is a universal answer, and don't land on every useful scrap with both feet. (Maybe you *can* find some items that you can tie together to see what works for you—but don't get carried away into thinking you can nail everything down to cause and effect and neatly dispense with it.) You can have the benefit of the insights without the nails. How many times in the history of science, for example, has a researcher leaped onto a phenomenon, explained the cause-and-effect relationship, and then gone on merrily about his or her business utterly convinced as to the "why" of how something worked? Years later, someone else has come along and blown the "why" sky high, but the "how" remained as true and as efficacious as it ever had been.

Psychology, to me, is an art, not a science. I think the two have much in common and much to offer one another. As Shakespeare said, "There are more things in heaven and earth, Horatio, Than are dreamt of in your philosophy."

Many things work for us and are used by us without our really understanding why: electricity, acoustics, and aspirin, for example. Someday we may understand more of the *why* about ourselves and our worlds, but meanwhile, we live on a lot of faith and trust while we strive to know more.

Can psychotherapy (or psychotherapies) help with depression?

The answer to that depends on the individual. In some cases, yes; in some cases, a qualified yes; in some cases, no; in some cases, a qualified no. It depends largely on luck, careful investigation before selecting your therapy, sufficient commitment to give it a try, or all three. There is no such thing as one animal named "therapy." Just as there is no such thing as one mood named "depression." You've got to unlump them and take the trouble to search out what can help you. And you've got to go into the search without expecting instant, miraculous transformation. If you're not willing to take a lot of trouble, the lazy thing to do, of course, is keep your depression. In which case you can leave it in one big, amorphous lump and not bother with it at all.

If therapy can help, how will it help?

Therapy can help you deal with your depression when you're sitting in the middle of your puddle. Therapy can also help you prevent yourself from splashing down into the puddle to begin with. But therapy is, as I have been saying, not just what you get when you go to the office of an M.D. or Ph.D. with the right credentials and sit on a chair or lie on a couch.

Therapy is anything and everything that you use to help yourself with. The common denominator is that *you* find and use whatever works for you.

Look at everything. Take it all in and try on what appeals to you. In the process, you'll be studying yourself —and, eventually, what you will come to know and understand is yourself. *If* you are an apt student.

You are a complicated subject. Fascinating, but complicated.

The world is a complicated place. Fascinating, but complicated.

You can live in the world confused by all the complication and befuddled by all you do not understand, or you can live in the world intrigued by the infinite variety and enchanted by the infinite possibilities.

Take heart and have the courage to go out to meet the complexities. They will not destroy you; they will enrich you.

CHAPTER 12

Aces in the Hole or How to Stack the Deck in Your Favor

"Okay," you say to me, "I've tried your short-term measures, your long-term nostrums, your minor leagues, your stimulants, and your rebellion. I'm willing to go on trying them until they grow on me. But have you got a little something up your sleeve for the meanwhile?"

Good question. I have a couple of aces up my sleeve for the times when you've tried the other nostrums and are still depressed despite everything.

The Ace of Diamonds

The ace of diamonds is a yardstick called By the Same Token. (If King Arthur could have a sword called Excalibur, the ace of diamonds can be a yardstick called By the Same Token.) This is how you wield it.

Repeat the following logical deduction:

I am in a Black Pit which feels like it will last forever.
If it can last forever, then "By the Same Token" something good can last forever.
If nothing lasts forever then, "By the Same Token" This too will pass.

161

Now you have wielded By the Same Token and measured the state you are in against it. The obvious conclusion is that you simply have to go through this bit of pain in order to get to the other side.

Deal yourself the next card.

The Ace of Hearts

The ace of hearts is a matter of acting with courage even when you don't have any.

Now you say to yourself:

> Although I feel like nothing good will ever happen to me again, and I am convinced that I shall never be happy again . . .
> I will proceed to act on an "as if" basis.

I will conduct myself and my affairs as if I were *not* feeling like death warmed over—as if I were not ready to throw in all the towels in Macy's bath shop—as if I were not utterly defeated. I will act as if everything is just fine.

I will fix dinner as easily as if I were a hot-plate chef in a cafeteria. I will listen to the kids' requests for funding as if I were the Ford Foundation. I will plan a party for my husband's business associates as if I were the President's Chief of Protocol. I will take care of all the demands being made on me as if I being totally competent only required about 25 percent of my attention, leaving the other 75 percent of me free to do whatever I wanted.

If you act as if something is easy, it becomes easy. If you act as if it's hard, it becomes hard. You convince yourself of what you can or cannot do. Right this second say out loud, "She's right; it *is* easy to act as if."

Acting on an "as if" basis leads to feeling on an "as if" basis, which leads to becoming what you have been "as if"-ing.

My explanation for this is that it is the same as what happens with pain—the neurons which conduct pain impulses to the brain (if they're not neurons, I am glad to stand corrected) are like footpaths through the wild underbrush. The first few times you walk through, you're beating a new path. But after you pass through this same area again and again using the same path, it becomes established. The path widens and is clear and unobstructed, making passage smooth and easy. In this way, pain can continue to be felt after the cause of it has gone, because the path is established and the impulses travel along the path out of a kind of habit. For example, acupuncture works by interrupting the path and blocking the passage of the pain impulse.

The ace of hearts will help you break a new path through the wild underbrush. By acting as if everything were fine and dandy, the way is being cleared for positive impulses. The more positive impulses you send scooting down the path, the broader and clearer it will become. This is how, in my opinion, the power of positive thinking works.

Now put your two aces together and you have a fairly good hand. The ace of diamonds is the premise:

If pain can beat a path and run on its own "By the Same Token," so can well-being.

The ace of hearts is the hypothesis:

If I act "as if" everything is going well, eventually I will begin to feel that it is.

You are holding two aces—let's see if you can improve your hand even more. Throw away the other bum cards you have been holding and draw three new ones. The dealer in this case is your friend and has stacked the deck in your favor! (The idea of having the deck stacked in your favor does you good all by itself.)

So you draw three more cards.

The Ace of Clubs

I will add this ace to the two I am already holding:

I will set myself three goals.
I will make plans and carry out projects to help me attain them.

While I am planning and carrying out my plans, I will remind myself of my premise and my hypothesis—my ace of diamonds and my ace of hearts—and I will soon hold onto them for dear life. I will have faith that soon I shall begin to feel the confidence that comes from holding three aces.

This is a very good hand in anybody's game, but since my friend is still dealing. I'll turn up the next card.

The Ace of Spades

My fourth ace in the hole is to get physically tired doing things I enjoy. I play tennis. I jog. I bowl. I swim. I go horseback riding. I go fishing. I hike. I sail. I ski. I ride my bike. I go dancing. I take long walks.

I'm not athletic?

Okay—I clean the house. I wash the clothes. I convert the light switches to dimmers. I chop down a tree. I refinish some furniture. I saw wood. I polish the car or my shoes or the silver or all three. Instead of riding the bus or taking the car, I walk to work and back. I walk up and down stairs instead of taking the elevator. I defrost the refrigerator. I run the dog. I put up new drapes. I launder the carpets. I build new bookcases. I rearrange my decor.

I can't do any of the above?

Okay—I simply do not allow myself to sleep for twenty-four hours, or until I finish reading *The Decline and Fall of the Roman Empire*—whichever comes first.

Whatever I have to do to do it, *I get physically tired*.

Lo and behold, you are now holding four aces. That ought to make you feel better. But guess what! You turn up another ace. I told you the deck was stacked.

The Ace of Trumps

I make a list of things I want to do but am too inhibited to do ordinarily. Akin to the list you made "in extremis" but not quite as all-out, this list might include things you haven't let yourself indulge in, like:

I go to a masseur or masseuse (dealer's choice).

I take flying lessons.

I buy a pound of fresh Iranian caviar (the largest eggs) and a bottle of Dom Perignon. Then I devour them both all by myself in front of the TV during the six o'clock news. (What with inflation, you can content yourself with red caviar and Asti Spumante.)

I fly to London for a weekend.

I have a pedicure.

I go to a porno movie by myself and eat popcorn.

I give a Kama Sutra party and invite everyone to "come as you are."

I plan an entire week's menu with *only* the foods I love best regardless of calories or nutrition.

And so forth. Because *you* have to make your list of things *you* would like to do but never indulge yourself in.

If you deal yourself these five aces, you're bound to win out over your downer—unless, of course, you find yourself playing against six deuces. In which case, since you're out to win and you're not averse to pulling a little something more out of your sleeve, there's the final card in the game. The Joker.

The Joker can be anything you want it to be. If you're holding one, you can use it any way you want and it can be anything you need at the moment. Basically, The Joker is your ability to laugh at yourself and at the human condition.

Not long ago I saw a news clip on TV about a young man who suffers so much from allergic reactions that he has to wear a face mask constantly. Any food he eats makes him ill, and he has to sleep out-of-doors. Additives, chemicals used in food processing, man-made fibers and materials are all culprits which are causing his body to be outrageously insulted.

When interviewed, he was asked how he managed to keep his sense of humor, and he replied, "If I didn't, I couldn't live."

The Joker is the only thing standing between him and doing away with himself.

Play The Joker often in combination with your other five aces—it's the most useful card in the deck!

PART III

Preventing Your
Depressions

CHAPTER 13

Prevention—
Several Different Ounces

It used to be that when I was feeling up, I always thought, "This time it will last . . . this time things are beginning to go the way I want them to and I won't ever have those hideous, down periods again. Or hardly ever."

Sooner or later something else would come along and knock me off my pins and straight back to the bottom of the well—but not after water. For a long time, I alternated between two poles, accepting the pit as payment for the pinnacle. Like everybody else, I consoled myself with expressions like: You can't know the heights if you don't know the depths, or You have to experience pain in order to know joy, and other such assorted rot. I even remember when I was around twenty years old looking forward to experiencing pain because I felt it would deepen me. I call this rot, because—while depression is painful, I don't believe it is necessary to the appreciation of happiness. In and of itself, depression does not scoop us out and leave us deeper. My capacity for joy may be in inverse ratio to my capacity for pain, but depression has precious little to do with my capacity. The experience of pain *may* lead to understanding—in which case it does deepen us. And if the experience of depression leads to understanding, then it, too, contributes to our depth as human beings. In both cases, it is what we do with the experience that determines its effect on us.

When I set out to balance things a bit (to mitigate the extreme downs I got into at times), I therefore did not feel I would be sacrificing one whit of my sensitivity or my capacity to feel joy or my depth of understanding. *Au contraire!* Depression doesn't equip you for anything. Struggling with it, however, can be very enlightening.

The best time to take preventive measures is when you are not feeling down—sort of like fire drill. You have to get ready for trouble while there is no trouble. And if your measures don't prevent trouble, at least they help you get out of the building in one piece.

Circumstantial depressions are highly preventable. Not in the sense that I can offer you a handy craft kit for spinning your own cocoon or a road map to a trouble-free island paradise—but because all of us know that we are bound to be in for some rough circumstances from time to time, and how we think about those circumstances makes the difference between "having a depression" or working out a problem.

The first thing you have to learn in order to prevent circumstantial depressions is not to get yourself mixed up with outcomes. Earlier in the book I said, "Get involved with outcomes," and I'm not repudiating that. But I want to explain the difference between "mixing yourself up with outcomes" and "getting involved with outcomes." To get involved with outcomes means to have an investment and to care whether something comes out heads or tails—to have something at stake. To mix yourself up with outcomes means to confuse *you* (your ego, your ability, your energy, your talent, your brains, your heart, body, and soul) with whether or not something succeeds. This is equivalent to the Wright brothers concluding that their first model didn't get off the ground because they were pedestrian.

You are you.
Your effort is your effort.
You remain you regardless of the outcome of your effort.
You are no less than you were because your effort fails.

You are no more than you were because your effort succeeds.

Repeat this catechism out loud in order to separate you from your effort:

I am me.
My effort is my effort.
I remain who and what I am regardless of the outcome of my effort.

Now let me tell you about why we have to make the separation.

I have seen it happen in business over and over again. Let's say that the marketing director of a mail-order company has an idea for a product that he thinks will sell a million. He prepares a campaign, gets everything ready, and right on schedule he mails his package out and sits back to wait for the response.

What he gets is zilch. It dies all over him.

Right away this guy is a bum, right?

Wrong.

He may be a bum, but not necessarily because this particular campaign failed. There can be many reasons why it bombed and his job is to find them out, not to write it off as having failed because he is a numbskull. When he finds out why it failed, he'll be a better marketing director than he was before.

The reverse is also true. If it had succeeded, his job would be to find out why, not just bask in the success. Take the story of another marketing director (the first guy's cousin Bernie) who developed a direct mail promotion for selling accident insurance. Bernie didn't do anything special or out of the ordinary, yet the results were spectacular! Bernie got the kind of response marketing directors dream of—there had not been anything like it in the history of his company. Bernie was an instant hero, and for the next eight years, his company sent out the identical package (afraid to change a hair on its successful head). But the strange thing was that forever after, they only succeeded in getting a very modest response. Bernie clung to his ever-diminishing heroic image and tenaciously sent out the same package year after year. Nobody knew

171

why it didn't work anymore (nobody had known why it worked in the first place), and finally, predictably, the response died altogether. Bernie, ex-hero turned bum, got the ax.

Along came Simon, the thinking man's marketing director, who stuck in his thumb to see if he could pull out the secret of the puzzling promotion which had now assumed the stature of the riddle of the Sphinx. Simon, our brainy friend, says to himself, "Instead of trying to figure out why the campaign has been failing year after year, let's look at why the original campaign worked so well."

Look at it he did, from every angle—but no answer presented itself. At last, Simon, dauntless and intrepid as a real hero should be, got a brainstorm and went to the library. He looked up the old newspapers from the time around which the original mailing package had gone out and discovered that a day or so after the mailing (just about the time the package was being received), there had been a terrible plane crash, and all the newspapers and newscasts had been filled with the horrible details of this disaster. All this just when the insurance offer reached its audience. That was why it had been such an enormous success! Bernie had nothing to do with it! The hero was obviously Simon, who figured it all out and changed the mailing piece immediately.

The moral of the story is that you must make your best effort and certainly care about whether it succeeds or fails. But your feelings about yourself must be wrapped up in making the effort, not in how it comes out.

This is something almost everybody gets confused about. I've noticed it in politics, particularly when the outcome of a given stance makes the perpetrator a hero or a bum regardless of what part chance and other contributing circumstances may have played. We all tend to judge the deed and the doer by the outcome. I think we must learn to look more closely at both in order to see the truth. You may not be able to change the world's bad habit of making quick, superficial assessments, but you can surely change your own. You *must* know the difference and you *must* judge your performance by your effort—not by the outcome. Otherwise you could spend your life waiting for a plane to crash so that you could be a hero.

It is my opinion that a too-easy success can cause as much or more pain than failure. The many young entertainers who "click" too soon and too easily (because they happen to encapsulate some taste which is hot at the moment) are cases in point. Not understanding why they have succeeded with so little effort, they cannot handle their success. It is not based on something real—or something which is a natural outgrowth of their effort—and therefore they are overwhelmed by what they rightly feel is the unreality of their success. This can be a very frightening feeling.

Separating yourself from the results of your efforts requires that you know yourself. You have to be honest in your appraisal of who and what you are, what your abilities and limitations are; which turf you should trot on and which you run poorly on. It seems incredible, but those of us who suffer from habitual depression manifest an inability to be honest about ourselves. And this dishonesty takes two forms: the mis-appraisal of what's wrong with us (we exaggerate) and the misappraisal of what's right with us (we minimize). Both kinds of faulty appraisal are damaging and both are dishonest—it doesn't matter which side of the ledger you cheat on. And please stop confusing this kind of dishonesty with modesty or self-effacement!

You must give up inaccurate evaluations of yourself, and recognize that you have been using this kind of dishonesty for a purpose: to lower the expectations others may have of you and to lower the expectations you have of yourself. You must learn to appraise your efforts honestly and with a certain detachment, *without blaming yourself*. When he was asked to conduct the work of a certain composer, the great conductor Toscanini refused, saying that he knew his limitations and that he was not at his best conducting that particular composer's work. Toscanini felt no shame in admitting that he had limitations. One of the reasons he was so great was that he took his limitations into consideration. If you are able to be honest about your strong points—and your weak points—you will know how to cut your failures and your losses and increase your successes and gains. But more important, you will be able to assess your efforts without false blame (when you fail) or insecure bewilderment (when you succeed). In addition you will prevent depression which can occur in either case.

You can also use preventive measures against habitual depression. Like the Streetcar Named Desire, the Omnibus Named Habitual can be seen ten blocks away. You have a well-established route that it travels, making its regular stops. In characterizing this baddie, I said that you set yourself up for it—meaning that you are standing there waiting for it. Obviously, your preventive measures for this one have to be ladled out before setup time. Remember the telephone call when your friend broke the dinner date? A straightforward but gentle "Yes, I do mind" from you could have prevented the whole thing! Which leads to the villain in the piece: very often it is what you *don't* say or do that makes you feel depressed.

Let's back up a bit on this one. Fear is what usually prevents you from saying or doing what you really want to say or do. Fear of someone else's reaction, fear that someone else will not like you or love you. But the sneaky part is that all too often by not saying or doing something simply because you fear someone else's reaction (I am not speaking of the inhibitions of a healthy conscience or advocating running rampant over other people's rights and lefts), you set yourself up for those identical reactions in yourself. In other words, you become angry with yourself. You dislike yourself. And presto—depression! Like magic. In trying to avoid anger, disapproval, and dislike, you turn them all loose on yourself. If you were expressing and experiencing your real reactions, you would be most likely to avert the very reactions you're afraid of. (I said avert, not *avoid*. Avoidance is usually a pack of trouble no matter which way you turn.)

If you can get over the terror of receiving a negative reaction, you'll be able to express yourself in a natural, easy manner. And you'll be absolutely amazed that people will actually *like* it. It may take them a second or two if they are not used to this kind of straightforward dealing from you, but then they will relax and enjoy it. They will like it for two reasons. First, it relieves them of the need to walk on eggshells around you, since they will feel that they can be straightforward back and you won't be destroyed; second, it relieves them because it tells them clearly where they stand—what's really what. These two things make for a comfortable relationship.

In a way, this ounce of prevention is just another ounce of honesty.

On the subject of honesty—when people first begin to catch onto the idea of the kinds of honesty I've been talking about in both these instances, they sometimes go bananas over it and run it into the ground. It's like hunting season—anything with long ears that isn't red gets shot at. By amateurs, that is. So a cautionary word or two may be necessary. Being honest is not open season on being brutal. It is not a license for telling anybody and everybody everything and anything that happens to traverse your mind.

I have noticed that when some people in therapy get the green light for being honest, they start making up for all those years when they were repressing their true feelings by letting go at anything within range. Okay, I understand that it may be necessary to let it all out in order to unblock the stuck passage. But frankly, I don't want anyone to let it all out on me. I'm not the one you were angry with then, and I don't want to be the one to have to hold the bag now.

So although I urge certain kinds of honesty, when you start opening up and being more honest about your feelings, try not to make up for lost time and past heartache by making your current lovers, friends, and family pay for your past reticence. It's not their fault. Really it isn't. And even if it were (I wish I could issue no-fault insurance for human relations; I'd make a fortune), *you can't get anything back now*. You have to start fresh.

Punitive payments for the past may, in some cases, be in order. But punitive payments can't last forever—no matter how huge the former debt or injustice. They don't really make up for the hurts or the losses of the past, and they don't make for happy, one-to-one relationships in the present.

For your own sake, refuse emotional alimony if you can. Turn down the punitive payments if they're offered. Make a new start. Nobody can recompense you for the past, but *you* can make it up to *you* for all the rest of your future.

CHAPTER 14

Help Is Not a Dirty Word

There's one word people don't mind saying but hate to yell. That word is *uncle*. I don't know where the expression "yelling uncle" came from or how it came to mean, "Help, I'm giving in," but it is not something any of us does easily. There comes a time, however, when you've got to be able to stand there and holler, whisper, or whistle, "Uncle." I am again recommending selectivity. This time you have to choose your direction, because, as any sailor will tell you, you have to yell according to which way the wind is blowing in order to prevent it from blowing back in your face. More about direction in a moment.

Not being willing to yell uncle, or having difficulty getting the word out of your throat altogether, is not a simple physiological problem involving a small windpipe or clogged throat. It has nothing to do with your vocal cords. The reluctance to ask for help which most of us experience has to do with not trusting other people.

Fine. Now let's go one step further back.

Trusting people starts with trusting yourself—trusting the fact that you are worthy of other people's attention and concern. If you don't feel worthy, how can you expect or hope or trust them to give it to you?

All these fine friends and spouses and lovers I've been advising you to talk things over with may not be available to you if you have trouble trusting anyone enough to rate someone as a real and true friend to begin with. "Then," you may have been saying to yourself, "I really have a problem. How can I have good talk and good listening if I don't have a real and true friend?" (I'm using the *friend* in the sense of the role your listener would play in this setting, not the literal relationship to you.) To answer that question first, you can talk to a shrink and have the best possible listening because shrinks have fewer axes to grind than even the best friend that God ever created—and besides, they are trained to see and hear down to the bottom of your pit. So you can talk to a shrink if you feel you have no friends. And just because you have no friends at the moment doesn't mean you won't have some in the future. Another trained and uninvolved listener is your minister, rabbi, priest, doctor, or family counseling service. These are all good directions for yelling if spouses, lovers, and friends present difficulties of their own.

I want to digress somewhat about this business of not having friends as it relates to the difficulty of yelling uncle. Both of these problems are related to loneliness, so we may as well knock off some relations with one or two digressions.

People usually experience loneliness and friendlessness as a result of not attempting to relate because of some sense of unworthiness—they are convinced that no one would find them interesting enough to bother with. If you feel you are not worthwhile, then it follows that you don't deserve the satisfactions of closeness. And you are also afraid that closeness might reveal all the things about you that are unlikable or unlovable. With this kind of reasoning, it is better, you conclude, to keep everyone at a distance—meaning *you* keep the distance between yourself and them as a protection. That way you will not be hurt or disappointed, right? Your reasoning sets up an equation that states: *Intimacy and closeness = Vulnerability and Exposure.* Whereas: Casualness and Distance = Protection and Security. This kind of higher mathematics leads to loneliness. Loneliness is a product of *distance,* not aloneness! Much more about this in chapter twenty when we consider loneliness all on its own. But the connection here is the one about feeling worthy of receiving help. The real problem lies in whether you feel you deserve help. A feeble, tiny, tentative, halfhearted mew for help reflects how little you feel you should get the attention you need and want and how little you really hope to receive it. The honest-to-God yell—the lusty, full-throated, unmistakable roar—is based on a strong self-image. Naturally, if you have a problem with making noise, you're not going to develop a thunderous roar and become king of the jungle overnight. Just keep it in mind as a long-range goal. Meanwhile, keep working on your talking and listening and keep developing your lungs (and other communication equipment) in any and all directions. There are, as I said previously, many directions. I have mentioned the talking and listening roles we may assign to shrinks. I have also skirted lightly over ministers and doctors and other professional counseling types. I have listed self-help books like this one which allow you to listen to a friendly, understanding voice without anyone knowing you are seeking help, and I have suggested reading in philosophy, fiction, poetry, and so on. I have also dealt with talking to friends, whether they be lovers, spouses, or plain. There is a time and place for each kind of direction, and you can frequently call out in several directions at the same time. You can, for example, use friends, professionals, and books in conjunction with one another to achieve a kind of triangulation. This is a means of zeroing in on a problem from three different sides at once, and sometimes it will afford you a better fix than if you were just trying to do your locating from one direction.

Friends and lovers and spouses are the most frequently usable sources of help. Here, again, there are differences. We've spent a good deal of time discussing friends in general, but now I'd like to go into a finer distinction and talk about friend-as-lover and friend-as-spouse.

Friend-as-lover is expected to care automatically and romantically about whatever bugs us. If you're lucky, they do. But that does not rule out the myriad possibilities for misunderstanding, competition, indifference, and self-preoccupation that may get in the way for *both* of you. Lover may not be into the friend bit. Lover may not be able to handle it, and you've got to be prepared for a certain letdown if you expect lover to be friend automatically. A crossroad may present itself and you may have to acknowledge that you cannot have both with this one. This is another juncture at which you have to examine your intentions in this particular relationship and then either turn right (away from the whole thing) or left (into a narrower road than the one you thought you were on). It is not impossible to leave lover out of the listening and talking you want to do. It's just difficult. Remember, you have other options, other directions to move in, so just because lover doesn't want to listen doesn't mean you're out of luck or out of lover!

Friend-as-spouse has had books written about it. Somewhere in the marriage contract it is written in invisible ink, "Thy spouse shall be thy best friend and stand by thee through thick and thin." Don't look for it in your contract, because, as I said, it's written in invisible ink. It's there, though, and everybody knows it's there! Well, everybody goes around acting as if it were there. I'll go along with "maybe it should be there." But even if it were or is or should be or let's put it in, sometimes it's not possible to make good on it. Sometimes we fail each other in important ways. Sometimes, no matter how much someone may want to make good on being there for you (and the more they love you, the more the failure hurts), they just can't give you what you need. People's constitutions are so different, their needs so varied, that all the good will and love in the world cannot always win the day. I hate to say this, really, because I'm a romantic and more than willing to believe that anything is possible, but sometimes what you need from your spouse just isn't there for you when you need it. This doesn't mean you have to go out (or stay in) and shoot yourself or strangle your spouse. It simply means: (1) you have to accept the fact, and (2) you have to find what you need elsewhere; and (3) you have to resist the temptation to blame your spouse for not being able to supply you; and (4) you have to assess whether or not this lack is ongoing and your need is ongoing; in which case (5) you eventually have to do something about it. I haven't mentioned that there are some spouses who withhold their loving care and attention because of hangups of their own. It can be there, but you feel you are not getting any. This, too, is a situation which can be corrected. In fact, it's possible for both of you to get help together and separately and end up having a pretty terrific thing going for you.

Friend-as-spouse cannot be taken for granted. If you've got it, hallelujah. If you haven't, it isn't the end of the world.

Back to your ability to yell. Without labeling it as such or being aware that this is what we are doing, all of us grouse almost constantly. At least 98 percent of this grousing passes unnoticed because it's about little irritations and frustrations that we encounter daily. The next time a friend calls you on the telephone, mark down on a piece of paper every instance of some form of complaint—you'll see what I mean rather quickly. So much in everyday living is aggravating, consternating, frustrating, irritating —things that don't work, things that you stub your toe on, things that need your attention when you don't have time to spare, red tape, stupidity, and carelessness that cost you time and trouble, and so on—that the body of any conversation is likely to be well salted with some form of grousing. This is because we have never gotten used to the way things work. We always expect things to go smoothly, and we expect people to behave sanely and intelligently. But smooth, sane, and intelligent *is the exception.* So grousing is the rule.

The trouble is that when you are really upset—way beyond grousing—and you start to let go at a friend, said friend cannot instantly distinguish your real trouble from your normal grousing. Said friend needs a couple of hints in order to tell that this is the special 2 percent that needs more than cursory responses.

What usually happens is that instead of raising a big red flag to announce that this is not run-of-the-mill grouse material, you become hurt and upset because your friend has not picked up your metaphor and is consequently not responding the way you want. You interpret this to mean that your friend is insensitive, selfish, and bored with you —and when in need, who needs a friend like that? This is when you have to learn to yell uncle. Uncle is a big, red semaphore that even the most nearsighted friend can read. *If you don't give a signal that is legible, you have no right to expect anybody to know that you're suffering and need help.* So you must learn not only to say the word, you must learn to yell it!

Please make a note of this and underline it with your pencil:

> When you need help, a metaphor will not suffice—
> you've got to use a semaphore!

Learning to holler (you can start with *uncle* or pick a word of your own) is a vital part of getting help. This is one of those things that is so obvious that a lot of people overlook it. Us sensitive types figure that others should be as sensitive as we are (and at least half as perceptive), and that they should not require a big red semaphore when we are signaling for help.

I don't care how sensitive and perceptive people are; you can't expect something as small and subtle as a metaphor to get spotted all the time. Granted, it can get spotted once in a while when things are relatively quiet and there is not a whole lot of competition for your friend's attention. But by and large, there is a whole lot else going on, and you have to realize that while your metaphor may seem huge and dramatic (even overdramatic) to you, it doesn't necessarily come across with that same impact.

Someone I know who has arthritis is very reluctant to give in to it in any way—reluctant even to admit it when she has pain. She makes little or nothing of it, which is admirable, and people just don't think of her as having any sort of problem whatsoever (which is the way she wants it to be).

Recently she was washing out a few clothes by hand and asked her young daughter to help her wring out a small pair of underpants. Her daughter muttered something about, "Oh, Mom, I've got my hands full of peanuts."

The woman, who was feeling considerable pain but had not mentioned it, expected her daughter to know instantly that she was in pain. The daughter *did* realize it a second later but had simply not been thinking about her mother's arthritic condition at that moment. Meanwhile, her mother was terribly upset and hurt because her muted plea for help had not immediately been picked up. How much easier if she had simply prefaced her request with an admission that her hands were bothering her and she would appreciate some help.

As delightful, as exquisite, as tremulously satisfying as you may find it to offer delicate subtleties and to have them grasped and appreciated, it is a form of self-indulgence which can be taken too far when you want or need to communicate something to someone. You can't afford to enjoy what you are thinking of as "subtle"—not when you need to communicate!

Why?

Because by the time your message leaves the tender confines of your psyche and starts to travel across the untrackable and unlimited space between you and the next guy, boy, does it get attenuated. Not to mention diluted. Or even lost in space altogether. Now all of this is relative —you may perceive your effort to communicate as subtle when in actuality it is inaudible. You are perceiving a yell as ear-shattering when in fact it is probably well within normal decibel range. *You are standing directly in front of the speaker* (since you *are* the speaker), so naturally the volume is hitting you at full blast. But by the time it travels even across the room (which can be the same as the other side of the moon sometimes), if often loses its immediacy. And if there's a lot of static, it may get lost totally.

Aside from yelling help or uncle, you'll discover that hollering is a very good thing to be able to do. This is when you can expand your yell vocabulary to a whole range of other words. You might like to yell *aiuto* for a change, like they do in Italian opera. Another good word to learn to yell is *stop*. You'd be surprised how many people can't say that word, let alone yell it. Generally, they are the same people who have trouble with the word *no* or the word *don't*. It may have something to do with the shape of their palates, or it may be that custom has eradicated these words from the vocabularies of certain groups, the way certain people learn to speak in particular ways for peculiar reasons. (i.e., Castilian Spanish is spoken with a lisp simply because King Philip II of Spain lisped and no one in his court wanted to offend him by speaking differently.)

182

In any case, if you practice learning to yell, it will develop your lungs and vocal cords, and eventually you will be able to project without feeling that you are yelling at all. Projecting is important when you want to get something across. You don't need a loudspeaker or a voice amplifier; you only need to project clearly and directly what you are really feeling across whatever distance there is between yourself and whomever you want to communicate with.

Projection is also required when you are talking to a shrink or other professional listener. Just because someone may be trained to listen, don't assume that all you have to do is flick an eyelid or silently mouth your message and it will get picked up. No way. Under all that training is another human being whose attention span is not unlimited, whose acuity is not perfect, and who may just happen to get tired or not feel up to snuff once in a while. It's not easy to maintain edge-of-the-seat listening hour after hour.

I have a sneaking suspicion that the main reason for our reluctance to yell for help is that the part of our brain that controls the yelling center *doesn't want help*. Don't put it past this part of your cerebrum to take some perverse pleasure in throttling your yell impulse. The reasons for this may be very devious indeed and bear examination with a professional.

Let us now consider what happens *after* you yell. You've yelled wholeheartedly, full-throatedly, and at length. You've perched on a telephone wire and sung your song for all to hear. You're a regular blue-jay when it comes to having a penetrating call that carries your message. Now what?

Someone *does* hear! Someone not only hears .. someone *responds!*

Hallelujah!

But wait a minute—that's not the end of it. Now it's back in *your* lap because now you've got to listen. Whoever the good soul was who heard you and responded has something to say, and now you have to listen to it. You have to hear it. You may not be able to digest all of it immediately, and it may take you quite a bit of time and practice before you are able to incorporate the good advice into your modus operandi. But remember that when your friend, lover, or shrink has heard you and then offers everything he, she or it knows on the subject, the offer in itself won't mash potatoes. *You've* got to do the work. You've got to apply it to your own hide and see if it works for you. Once you discover what does work for you, then, dear, weary soul, you've got to apply it over and over again until it becomes second nature. Sorry about that, but I'm not offering instant and magical panaceas which work without your having to lift a finger. Neither will anyone else; if someone does, look out!

I have to make a small confession, and that is that I love work. Sigmund and I agree that the two most important things in life are love and work. If you're not into either one and don't want to be, tear off the back cover of this book and send it to me along with twenty box tops from your Valium package and I'll give you a refund. Personally.

If you have simply never gotten into the joy of work or love, then maybe we can find a way to help you give them a try. Open up and give it *all* a try. You have nothing to lose except your depressions.

I hope it didn't escape you that I said, "Once you discover what does work. . . ." This is based on first listening to everything at least once through. Since you did the yelling for help, you're obliged to listen. But you can't expect that everything you hear is going to be your made-in-heaven answer. After you listen, you consider (like you did with your boulder)—and if it sounds feasible, then you try it to see if it works for you. No matter how good the advice you receive may be, it may not work for you. You can only find out by trying.

Then again, part of what you are offered may work, but not all. The coati is a wonderful little animal somewhat resembling a raccoon. It has a long, flexible snout and elegant little fingers with which it examines, with infinite care, every piece of food that comes its way. I suggest that you use this delightful creature as a role model! Examine every piece of advice with infinite care, turning it over and over, this way and that, comparing it to your other pieces of lettuce and finally to your several carrots. At long last, you, like the choosy coati, will select the piece of advice that looks the best to you, and you will devour it delicately.

Oh, the satisfaction of feeling that you have made a really considered choice. Delicious!

To sum up: if you want help, first, yell for it; second, listen to it; third, try it out and see if it suits you; and fourth, when it does, put it on your regular menu.

There are some dishes you can eat every day of your life. There are some dishes you enjoy every once in awhile. There are some dishes you loved when you first tried them, but you change. You're not accepting something forever just because you tried it out. Allow yourself to keep the option of changing your menu when your tastes change or when you find things that suit you better.

Those things that suit you to a "t" may still require a little time before they become second nature. You'll need some patience, so I will offer you two exercises to help you develop it. They are designed to give you an appreciation of the beauty of slow as opposed to fast. I call them my antinuclear age devices.

1. At least once a day, spend some time staring at the minute hand of your clock. Try to see it move. (Do not use a clock with a second hand.) This will teach you that things do move and are moving whether or not you perceive the movement.

2. Get yourself a plant, preferably a very small plant. Watch it grow every day—day to day, week to week. month to month. This teaches the same lesson but is slower still. Things grow and develop at their own pace and cannot be hurried.

Finally, think about things moving slowly. Think about how beautiful it is that they are moving continually all the time even though you can't see it happening. Think about how you count on things that you can't see happening, and how much faith and trust that takes. Faith and trust are the hardest tenets of any belief. But you already have faith and trust in yourself or you wouldn't be able to function at all.

All you have to do is build on what you already have.

CHAPTER 15

Point of View About Living or How to Make a Rose Garden out of Your Nettles

At a crucial point in my life, I got to thinking about what the foundations of happiness in life are, and I boiled them down to four basic pillars:

home
livelihood or income
love
work

Since then, I have always been able to rate my happiness (or unhappiness) according to how many or how few of the four basics I have at any given time. The lowest point of my life was once when, for a brief period, I only had about half of one.

As I set about trying to acquire the other three and a half, I discovered that the only way I could keep from succumbing to total depression was to concentrate on one and only one at a time. Little by little, I gained ground and improved my lot.

For a brief period once, I had three and a half at the same time—but I have never had all four simultaneously.

I think if I ever do manage to have all four together. I will be totally happy.

Of course, the absolute ideal is having all four and combining them so that you are sharing your home with the one you love and are earning your livelihood by doing the work which gives your life purpose and meaning.

Do you know anyone whom you consider to be truly happy? If so, I'll lay you odds that he or she is doing just that; at any rate, the ones I know are.

There's happiness to be had not only in having all four, in the getting. Assess your situation. Which of the four do you have right now? Write it or them down. Now write down the one(s) you lack. In my experience, you can survive briefly with just one or a fraction of one.

If you lack more than one, first go after the one you can get with the greatest relative ease. Plan your campaign just as you do when you have any obstacle to overcome—it's the same type of technique.

Let's say that your list of missing pillars shows that a home is missing, love is missing, work is missing, but you have three-quarters of a livelihood. Sounds dismal, but it needn't be. The easiest of the missing pillars to acquire is a home, so start with that. Now the reason you probably lack a home is that you have been waiting for love to appear or for your livelihood to blossom out to a full, round one. *You must not insist on acquiring any one of the pillars in an ideal state right off the bat.* You can have a home in a shack or a one-room apartment—it doesn't have to be a mansion. Begin with four walls, make it a home; make it cozy and livable and plan to acquire the mansion later. The only thing you need to do in the beginning is make sure that the potential is there—otherwise whatever you do is a waste of time.

This is true of all the basic pillars—if the potential is there, you will set out to improve them when and how you can. It's fun and exciting to work on something to improve it, to enlarge it, to refine it, to decorate it. Even love relationships can be enhanced by the challenge of making them better and more satisfying to both parties. Given your nature, you may tend to hold back from things you could have because they have not, like Athena, sprung at you perfect and fullblown from the forehead of Zeus.

Very seldom have I gotten anything I really wanted *without much effort*. Sometimes I fantasize about apples dropping into my lap from the tree I'm sitting under with my mouth open, or the silver platter I've heard about that some people get things handed to them on. But I also know that I value what I do get because I have to work so hard to get it. As a result, I don't know what being jaded feels like and I can get enormous pleasure out of the most ordinary thing.

People who have things handed to them seldom deeply enjoy what they have. And that is the worst deprivation of all. They evidence their discontent. They are confused about what is valuable or important. They can't take real pleasure, because without an investment from them, the payoff is a hoax. This is why they feel cheated . . . and rightly so. This is why so many rich or successful people who have gotten what they have too easily are miserable and unhappy and bored. This is why so many of them are driven to get more . . . more . . . more . . . because there is no satisfaction. This is what causes "success nymphomania"—lack of basic satisfaction.

Actually, the best way to attain happiness is to decide what you want. Plan how to get it. Work like hell. And then savor your reward to the fullest.

Undoubtedly, while you are in the process of working to attain your pillars, the times of down will come. You will glance upward and feel discouraged by the fact that you've only made an inch of progress on one tower in the last six months. Let me tell you that an inch can be one of the biggest gains you'll ever make—if it is in the right direction! You have to learn to stroke yourself in regard to progress. Make yourself a perspective square and view your accomplishments, not in terms of how far you still have to go, but in terms of how far you've already come. Once you've made that first inch, you've got living proof that it's possible.

The pace can feel killingly slow—imperceptible, in fact (like the minute hand moving). This is when you need landmarks. When you feel that things are moving too slowly or not at all, remind yourself of what the terrain looked like when you set out. Then take heart and pride in that first all-important inch. Rejoice in the pillars that you already have (even if they are partials), admire your achievements inch by inch, and offer yourself the praise that you deserve.

Most of us keep "blame accounts" on our activities. At the drop of a hat, we can recite all the things we ever messed up on or felt a failure at. How many of us keep "praise accounts," however? If you're going to berate yourself for everything that's wrong in your life—for all the mistakes, goofs, self-destructions and carelessness you feel liable for—then why not keep note of all the good things you do for yourself? Why not tear up the blame accounts and start to praise yourself where it is deserved?

There are lots of things you can do that are worthy of praise. Have you quit smoking? or started exercising? or taken off a little weight? or read a book you've been meaning to read? or cut down on your caffeine intake?

When I started my praise campaign, I began to enjoy doing things that were good for me so much that I looked around to find at least one good thing to do each day. No matter how small it might be, it gave me satisfaction to know that I had something to place in the plus column for the day—doing the laundry, polishing shoes, throwing out unneeded papers, sewing on missing buttons, riding my bicycle, and so on. The idea is to give yourself things to feel good about instead of bad about. It sounds simple, but for us self-knockers, one of the hardest things is to give ourselves just praise.

If you have trouble with the word *enough*, let me offer a substitute. Try saying, "So far, so good." This is part of learning to be pleased with the littlest thing you can manage rather than remaining full of self-loathing for all the big things you can't manage. When you feel like crawling around on your belly, vacuuming your house can be a tremendous accomplishment. *Aim low when you feel low*. That inch I was talking about that gets you back on the right track is actually a giant step. You don't have to cover a mile at each stride. The tiny space between a negative act and a positive act is an incalculably large distance. This is where "So far, so good" comes in. It is enough to cross that huge distance, so as you gain your inches, you should give yourself praise. You don't have to be permanently satisfied, but you have to be pleased by and for each step in the right direction.

Everybody knows the story of half-full versus half-empty. Happiness or misery resides in your attitude. I used to make myself miserable by looking at an isolated event and finding it disappointing. Nothing was ever enough. I was never content to say "So far, so good." Then someone pointed out to me that most endeavors are a *process*. They are ongoing developments which require ongoing investments and efforts. Progress must be measured in terms of movement in a direction—not ultimate destination.

If you stop to think about it, you will realize that your ultimate destinations change along the way anyhow. During the process, you learn from and are affected by events. You make corrections and adjustments. All these minute changes alter your course and can even change your course completely, because you are discovering and refining as you proceed.

We may start out thinking we know exactly where we are headed (and many people do make a beeline for their goal without any detour). But many more of us make shifts that lead to a different destination altogether. A friend of mine worked for the same company for twelve years, earning himself a fine reputation and the position of associate director. Everyone believed that when the director retired, George would, of course, be promoted. George thought so too. He attended board meetings and was aware of being groomed to succeed by the director himself. But George was also aware of having his own style, which was somewhat more free-wheeling and imaginative than that of the older director. He recognized that the board was looking for a continuation of the status quo, while George had a number of innovative ideas he was anxious to put into effect when he took over the helm.

Although my friend had gone into the business thinking that his ultimate goal would be directorship, the experiences and self-knowledge acquired along the way led to a reexamination of his goal and ultimately to a major shift. When the director finally retired, George searched himself very deeply and made a decision to quit and go into business for himself. He has never been happier, and has made even more of a success than he would have as director of a company which would have hamstrung him and thwarted his best efforts.

It is fine to have a goal and to strive toward it. But you should keep in mind that striving is only a process—and that you must remain open and receptive toward new ideas and growth.

From this it is one small step to seeing living as a process, and to granting yourself the pleasure, praise, and rewards of each step you take in the right direction.

Your attitude dictates how you perceive things. You will feel defeated or challenged by problems according to how you perceive your ability to work out solutions. As I said earlier, we all have limitations, and it is important to recognize them. But knowing your limitations involves realistic assessments of your abilities, not fearful retreats.

There is no such thing as life without pain, loss, failure, and defeat. Neither you nor anyone else is going to get through life without these and more nettles. You may not see the other person's nettles—and this can be because you view as successful someone who has learned to *use* his nettles, or at least to accept them along with the soft stuff.

All those hard, prickly, thorny things like nettles and spurs serve a purpose in nature. They are there to protect fragile growth. They are there to prevent clumsy hands and stumbling feet from tearing up and crushing heedlessly. You might say that nature gives you your thorns and nettles to get you to pay heed, too. To get you to pay careful attention. To remind you that beautiful things are rare and delicate and evanescent—that they must be cared for and not taken for granted. They are there to teach you to hold dear, touch tenderly, treat reverently, respect and cherish and value what is fragile in yourself. Beautiful things are hard to come by, and I believe that the nettles that get in your way are a means of slowing you down and making you treat the beautiful things within yourself with respect.

Your efforts come out of a beautiful, fragile, vulnerable place inside yourself. And your nettles must help you learn to revere and respect your efforts and your goals. When you evaluate the difficulty of a goal properly, you will be able to appreciate properly the *efforts toward attaining it* separately from the *achievement of it*. This is the philosophy which says that it is the struggle that is important, not the attainment. The means, not the end.

If Sisyphus' * goal had been to develop his back, shoulder, arm, and leg muscles, he would not have felt like a martyr every time the rock rolled back down the hill. He would have felt pleased at having had a good workout. Buy Sisyphus a sweat suit, and you will immediately turn a pessimist into an optimist. Sisyphus was condemned by his attitude, not by his occupation!

Our attitudes are often directed by the signs that are placed on things. These signs are a kind of insignia, which elicit a predictable reaction from us. I think it is worthwhile to think about how our response to a given action varies according to the circumstances and the context (or "insignia") of the situation.

Action	With Proper Insignia	Without Insignia
killing	heroism and duty	murder
not eating	fasting	starvation
fighting	sport	violence
mental exertion	games	work
hurting animals	scientific experiment	cruelty
risking money	business venture	reckless gambling
running	exercise	flight
surrendering life	martyrdom	suicide
performing in public	show business	exhibitionism
cooking	hobby or art	chore or drudgery
nudity	sexiness	lewdness

* In Greek mythology, Sisyphus, a cruel King of Corinth, was condemned to roll repeatedly a huge stone up a hill only to have it rush back down just before reaching the peak. His punishment in the underworld was one of the sights Virgil described in *The Aeneid*.

The list could go on and on. Clothes, labels, flags, decorations, tags—all of these are insignia. But perhaps the most important insignia are the words we attach to our actions. Your attitudes are attached to the things you or others do by the words which are assigned to the actions.

Words are mental signposts which you follow. They set you up for how you think about a given thing. You are free to assign or not assign an insignia as you choose—and you may consistently assign a *negative* insignia to actions that should be viewed as *positive*. In other words, if you invite a friend over for dinner, you may choose to view cooking as a hobby and an art, or as a chore and a burden. You can readily see how the insignia you place on an act affects (and is affected by) your attitude. I know a woman who feels that nudity is lewd all the time; she actually admits that she feels ashamed when she gets undressed to take a bath.

Make your own list of the actions with which you have negative associations. Include everything you dislike, hate, abhor, resent, are irked by, find irritating, resist doing, or avoid if you can. Then try your level best, intellectually, to fill in the column of proper insignia—the signs that can be attached to make each of the very same items positive.

By the mere act of seeking a positive insignia for something you find distasteful or difficult, you will see how your attitudes can be conditioned toward the good, just as they were conditioned at some point in the remote past to the bad.

After you get the hang of looking for positive insignia (both external and internal), take the same list you started with—the list of negatives—and see what you can do to begin attaching as many positive signs to them as possible. For example, if you detest cooking as a chore and you have already labeled it a hobby, then go out and buy yourself a fancy, funny apron and a big chef's hat to wear when you're cooking. Wear your sweat suit to clean the house. Carry your groceries home in your bowling bag.

The internal signals are the words and labels you use to describe your action. Instead of feeling that the household budget is demeaning, how about looking at it as a game of numbers, a kind of monopoly for real.

It's what you tell yourself that matters.

If you feel depressed because you can't afford to dine out in an expensive restaurant, blow a little money on something exotic that you can fix at home. There are always things you can have and enjoy if you think of them that way. If you have a taste for designer clothes but can't afford the prices, then label yourself as an innovator and dress with inventiveness and imagination. Design your own combinations and your own off-the-beaten-track look. Fashion and tastes are changing constantly, and you can be one step ahead if you have the desire and the attitude of a pacesetter. Go to the library and look over all the books on costume and fashion from earlier periods. Check out old magazines. Modes in dress come and go, and you can use the old to inspire you to something new.

Pacesetters and trendmakers are people who capitalize on their imaginations. They establish a reputation for being creative, and the world follows their lead because it's safe. If you are not afraid to think for yourself, to use your imagination and creativity, you can turn any nettle into a spur to positive action. Free your attitudes and your imagination will follow suit.

You can literally choose how you view anything: *nobody can impose a negative, self-defeating attitude on you*. Since the choice is yours, opt for a view with room—room to be happy, room to change, room to enjoy life, room to open, to accept, and to grow. Room for others. And room for yourself.

Just remember, a nettle ain't nothin' but a rose's bodyguard!

CHAPTER 16

Depression and Overindulgence in All Those Good Things Like: Eating, Drinking, Smoking, and Worrying

In the last chapter, I accused you of having trouble saying the word *enough,* which isn't surprising when you consider how heavy it is. The word *enough* is loaded: it implies satisfaction—having one's needs, desires, wishes, hungers, wants, appetites, and yearnings fulfilled.

Not bad, eh? Not if you could get it.

Do you know anyone who has enough? Who is satisfied? If you do, in most cases, either they are too unimaginative or dull to think up new things, they are dead, or they are kidding themselves—so don't buy it. Everybody still wants *something.* You may be satisfied in one area or more, but there are always other areas and needs—there are always the recurring wants that clamor to be refilled and replenished repeatedly. So I return to my accusation that, in all likelihood, you have trouble with *enough*—trouble feeling satisfied.

And so does nearly everybody else. Now let's examine what *you* do about it.

195

A popular shrink term is *compensation*—if you don't have a yo-yo, you can take off on your skate board; if you don't have enough love, you can have three desserts; if you feel like a ninety-pound weakling, you can bully your kid sister; if you have a low sex drive, you can wear lots of makeup and low-cut dresses (or outmacho Tarzan and try to make every body in town).

The framework I'm putting you into is the *habit* of substituting one kind of satisfaction for another. If you look around, you'll see that our entire society is hooked on substitution: saccharin for sugar, plastics for wood and metal, nylon and rayon for silk, polyester for wool, chemical dyes for natural color, and so forth. Lately, we seem to be getting into a lot of trouble with these substitutes—the things you use to eliminate 150 extra calories give you cancer.

As with almost everything—depending on how you use it—substituting can be helpful or harmful. You've heard about rebellion by constructive substitutes and manipulation by constructive substitutes. Now I want to explore the relationship between *habits* and *satisfaction*, in the hope of showing you how you can learn to use substitutes for your bad habits.

Habits

What is a habit? James L. Mursell in his book *How to Make and Break Habits* defines a habit as a "standardized pattern of learned behavior." He calls habits "tools for living," and explains their function as "techniques for dealing with some life problem . . . a method of trying to achieve some *definable satisfaction*." (My italics.) In other words, they are "routines with a purpose."

How do you form a habit, and why do you form a particular one rather than a different one? If a habit is serving some purpose and giving you some kind of satisfaction, obviously the purpose and the need existed, and you looked around for some means of assuaging it. Consciously or unconsciously, you tried a number of different methods until you discovered the one that worked best for you. For example, the person who feels insecure may constantly acquire things in an attempt to satisfy the need for security. In this way, buying becomes a habit which is satisfying a need (but only for a moment, which is why it must be repeated over and over again). I know someone who almost always asks, when she calls on the phone, "Bad time?" This habit satisfies her need to be considerate and at the same time insures that she will not ever continue an unwelcome or untimely conversation. She is protecting herself from a possible rejection situation (another method of satisfying the need for security). In this case, her habit is a good one since it serves its purpose and does no one any harm.

I mention these two habits first because I want to make it clear that smoking, drinking, and eating are not the only habits people develop to answer other needs. They are the ones most people concern themselves with, but I think it is necessary to understand and recognize the basic *system* that is at work. Then you will be in a position to cope with any or all of the habits that you decide are bad for you.

High up on this list, as far as I am concerned, is the habit of becoming depressed. According to our definitions, becoming depressed habitually is:

1. a standardized pattern of learned behavior
2. a tool for living
3. a technique for dealing with some life problem
4. a routine with a purpose

In order to change or control any habit, first you have to understand how you are using it and why: what purpose is it serving? What are you getting out of it? So we have to begin by facing the problems that are behind the habit. Suppose you have a habit of always being late for appointments. You have to sit yourself down and scrutinize *why*. Don't just pass it off as "that's the way I am," and be done with it. There are reasons, and until you discover what your reasons are, you'll go on being late. These reasons can be quite different for each individual. For one person, it may be a reluctance to do whatever is scheduled; for another, it may be a punitive measure against a particular person; it may be indifference to or lack of respect for others; it may be arrogance or fear; resentment or anger, and so on. Only you can find out the real purpose your tardiness is serving . . . by confronting yourself solidly with the question, "Why?" Once you find the answer, you will be able to deal directly with the real problem and eliminate the need for the habit which you have substituted to take its place. More important, when you discover the underlying problem, you can devise ways of making your constructive substitutes work for good ends—you can turn bad habits into good habits.

So look for the meaning behind your habit; look for the reason you do it.

For example, it is my conviction that hypochondria, as the body's way of giving you the okay to goof off, is a habit that serves several interesting purposes. By not feeling well, you don't have to do certain things that you don't want to do. By not feeling well, you also lower your own (and other people's) expectations of you. You can readily see how destructive a habit like this can be when you realize that your body has had to go to such lengths to supply you with a viable excuse. I find it so sad that people must actually become sick to relieve the pressure on themselves! How much better to get to the root of the problem and deal directly with that.

I know someone who gets the runs when she feels trapped by something; someone else who developed terrific pains in the arms when he felt incapable of lifting a finger to overcome a situation he couldn't tolerate; someone else who gets nauseous in response to things she can't stomach, and another person who gets muscle-tension headaches when the kids are a pain in the neck. The list could go on and on. How many of these have you experienced? How many have expressed unconscious reactions to disturbing situations? Try making up a list of as many other expressions as you can think of that describe psychological reactions in physical terms. I think you'll find it very interesting!

The parallel I am making is this: what is it that you eat, drink, smoke, and become depressed about instead of?

I'll never forget the time I discovered this business of "instead of"—I was busy telling my shrink about an elaborate plan I had hatched for handling a certain issue with my lover. Under certain circumstances I would do "this" but under other circumstances I would do "that." I developed an elaborate game strategy for handling all possible reactions, but none of my fancy footwork had anything to do with confronting the real issues in the relationship . . . I was only concerned with maneuvers. When I finished my recitation and was feeling quite pleased with my cleverness, she looked me straight in the eye and asked, "What are you doing all that instead of?" The entire edifice crumbled at my feet, and for the first time, I saw what I had been doing.

Once you see what you have been doing and recognize *why*, you can start to use your brain to reorganize your means of answering your purpose—to devise better ways of achieving the satisfactions you want. You don't have to break a bad habit—you have to reorganize it!

Something has caused me to form the habit (the need that wants satisfaction) and something has caused me to maintain it (the satisfaction I get from it). Let's examine how some of our basic habits work as a system and take a stroll through some "instead ofs" in the common bad habit area, with acknowledgment to Dr. R. D. Laing for the use of the term "knots."

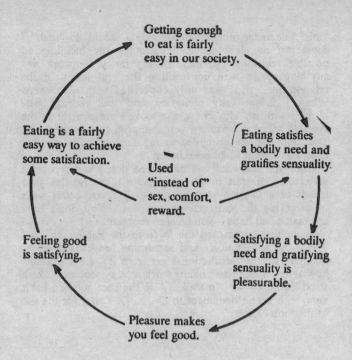

The Eating Knot

It is commonplace to view overeating as an "instead of" for other bodily needs and for the gratification of sensuality (i.e., sex). Overeating, however, may be an "instead of" for other satisfactions as well. It is not cut and dried, and no one can assign a cause to anyone else. You've got to figure it out for yourself. The "instead ofs" I suggest may or may not suit your situation. If they don't, try to determine which ones do.

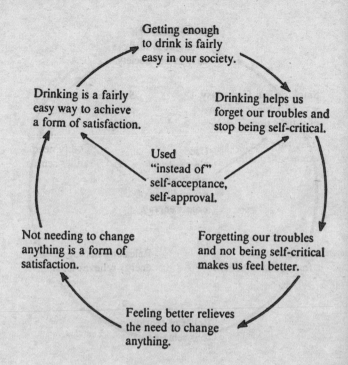

The Drinking Knot

As you look over the knots, remember that the satisfactions I have assigned to one bad habit might be applied to another. There are many common attributes and many similarities in the nature of the needs that are being served and the means of serving those needs. I emphasize the *system*—the dynamics of the knot habits, rather than the specifics.

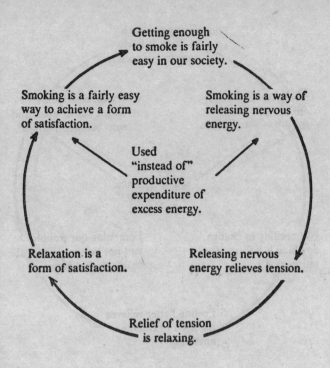

Getting enough
to smoke is fairly
easy in our society.

Smoking is a fairly easy
way to achieve a form
of satisfaction.

Smoking is a way of
releasing nervous
energy.

Used
"instead of"
productive
expenditure of
excess energy.

Relaxation is a
form of satisfaction.

Releasing nervous
energy relieves tension.

Relief of tension
is relaxing.

The Smoking Knot

One element common to the Eating, Drinking, and
Smoking knots is the play or recreational aspect. They
serve the purpose of entertainment (as does the Worrying
Knot) in addition to their other purposes.

Finding enough to worry about is fairly easy in our society.

Worrying gives you something to think about.

Thinking about something is a distraction.

Distractions are entertaining.

Entertainment is a form of satisfaction.

Worrying is a fairly easy way to achieve a form of satisfaction.

Used "instead of" constructive planning.

The Worrying Knot

The Worrying Knot might also be called the Entertainment Depression Knot.

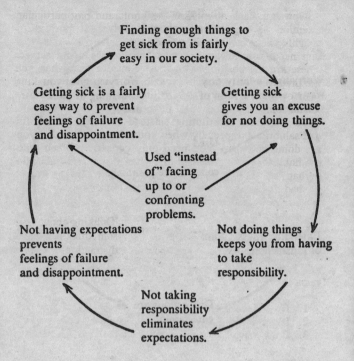

Finding enough things to get sick from is fairly easy in our society.

Getting sick is a fairly easy way to prevent feelings of failure and disappointment.

Getting sick gives you an excuse for not doing things.

Used "instead of" facing up to or confronting problems.

Not having expectations prevents feelings of failure and disappointment.

Not doing things keeps you from having to take responsibility.

Not taking responsibility eliminates expectations.

The Getting-Sick Knot

The Getting-Sick Knot differs from the others in that rather than supplying you with the ability to achieve a substitute satisfaction, it supplies you with a substitute for your dissatisfaction.

Now look back at each of the knots and pay particular attention to the second and third statement positions—roughly two o'clock and four o'clock. Two o'clock is what you need; four o'clock is what *purpose* is being served. These are the positions you must consider *first* when you are preparing to reorganize your habit. So begin by making your own set of knots—the habits you want to reorganize—and think through each of the positions.

To a degree, substituting "instead ofs" can be helpful and salubrious, especially when you are aware of what you are doing and why. You need only concern yourself with the habit that is an "instead of" when it is a *bad* habit. So perhaps we should define what a bad habit is. A habit can be bad because it doesn't serve the purpose very well, because the purpose is an undesirable one, or because the habit only reinforces the need it is supposed to serve. What may be a bad habit for one person may be an innocuous habit for another. It is always you *in relation to* the habit that determines whether it is good, bad, or indifferent. So ask yourself these three questions about each knot you think may be bad for you:

1. Does it serve my purpose as well as it might?
2. Is my purpose one that I want to be served?
3. Does my habit do me more harm than good?

If your habit is a bad one or only an indifferent one, you may find that there are better tools for dealing with your problem—tools that are more efficient or have no drawbacks. Some habits stick with you simply because you haven't thought out what you're using them for and therefore have not considered any other way of answering your need. You've been doing something a certain way (it's a habit) and you just haven't thought about doing it any other way. There are always alternatives, and if you discover a solid reason for giving up one habit, you can probably find a better way to satisfy whatever need it served. You must have a really sound reason for wanting to switch, however, so be clear about why you reach the conclusion that you need to trade in the old habit for a new one.

The real point of writing down your knots is to get you to think through what you are doing and why. A friend of mine recently commented that I was very definite about what I wanted and what I didn't want, what I liked and what I didn't like. In thinking it over, I agreed. Strangely enough, I had not really thought about it before, and it had only vaguely occurred to me that a great many people are not at all sure of what they want. My friend feels that, in fact, most people do not know what they want. If this is true, it may be why so much "instead of-ing" takes place. If you don't know what you want or need, naturally you'll take something (anything?) that will give you some kind of satisfaction. It seems clear that the hardest wants to satisfy are the ones you don't know exist!

Therefore, let us employ a *wantfinder*, a sort of radar for detecting your desires, needs, and wants. If you can identify them, maybe you can find substitutes for the satisfactions you are using that are behavioral bad habits.

WANTFINDER

This is what I need or want	This is the problem that is caused by lacking it	This is the behavioral bad habit I use to deal with my problem	This is the satisfaction I get from my behavioral bad habit
security	anxiety, fear	buy compulsively, behave rigidly	comfort from being surrounded by things, illusion of safety
love	self-hate	pursuit, courting, flattering, buying goodwill	a false self-image of being warm and appealing and lovable

This is what I need or want	This is the problem that is caused by lacking it	This is the behavioral bad habit I use to deal with my problem	This is the satisfaction I get from my behavioral bad habit
success	loss of self-respect	playing politics, cultivating those in power, being a "yes" person	a sense of being "in," of playing the game, of feeling like a winner and being clever
self-esteem	cynicism, bitterness, feeling misunderstood, self-loathing, feelings of inadequacy	blow my own horn, boss or bully others, insist on always having control, put myself down	a false sense of power, illusion of importance, defense against attack

This is only a suggestion of a list that you might draw up—an idea of how to be thinking of your own Wantfinder list. I must reiterate the point I have made a number of times already: neither I nor anyone else can do your thinking and figuring out for you. The examples I give are only to illustrate what I am talking about—to communicate the principle behind the method of self-help that is being offered. You must do the work! You must do the figuring out and applying of the principles to your own situation and personality. None of the suggestions I make is intended as dogma; they are worthless *unless* you use them as points of departure.

So it will be necessary for you to really dig out your own correlations and compensations as well as your own needs. First find out what you are doing and why. Then you will be ready to reorganize the bad habits so that you are getting the satisfactions you need from good habits.

As you can see, the problems caused by lacking what you need contribute to the feelings that underlie states of depression. Anxiety, fear, self-hate, loss of self-respect, cynicism, bitterness, self-loathing, feelings of inadequacy—these are all constituents of habitual depression. And of all the bad habits you might be heir to, habitual depression is likely to be the worst. I have deliberately not given you a Knot of Habitual Depression or put it as such on the Wantfinder list because it is a compendium of unanswered wants and needs. And because any one of your bad habits can be associated with habitual depression.

As you reorganize your system of satisfactions toward positive, self-enhancing behavior, I firmly believe that you will gain ground in preventing habitual depressions. The final step, then, is the selection of a good new habit that will give you the satisfaction you need in a way which is not harmful to you. Again, only as an illustration of what kind of things you might find to substitute, I will give examples for each of the needs and wants on the Wantfinder List:

security	instead of buying compulsively	put yourself on a budget and bank 15% of your net income each month
love	instead of pursuing, courting, wooing, flattering, and buying goodwill	accept yourself; like and/or love others without expectation of a return
success	instead of playing politics, cultivating those in power, saying yes to	make a comprehensive goal plan with detailed step-by-

| success (*continued*) | everything, compromising your standards | step moves toward your ultimate objective. Work hard to achieve it. Hold onto what you believe in even at the cost of being different |
| self-esteem | instead of blowing your own horn, bossing or bullying others, always insisting on having control, putting yourself down | examine yourself as honestly as you can and try to discover who and what you really are. Be *you* and let others be themselves. Enjoy the differences. |

Eating, drinking, smoking, and worrying can have a place in the natural course of living and are not, in themselves, necessarily bad habits. The problems with anything you do repetitively occurs as a result of over-burdening the satisfaction factor—forcing it to carry a different, heavier load, relying on it to bring you satisfactions of a more meaningful nature than those for which it was originally designed. When you force a simple pleasure or recreational habit to fill the nooks and crannies in between the letters of the word *enough*, you begin to abuse, corrupt, and distort the benefits you should be deriving. This is when you begin to overindulge, overdo, use to excess—and the simpler satisfaction you might have gained is lost to you, while the inadequacy of the bad habit—in giving you real satisfaction—becomes a new source of depression.

Habits have no innate ability to keep you in their thrall. The only reason they persist is that they are offering some satisfaction, serving some purpose, answering some need. You allow them to persist by not seeking any other, better form of satisfying the same needs. Every habit, good or bad, is acquired and learned in the same way—by finding that it is a means of satisfaction. If you smoke because you need to relieve tension, you may discover that certain physical exercises can accomplish the same purpose; if you drink to escape from your anxieties, you may find that learning judo will give you self-confidence. If you overeat because you feel deprived of the comfort of love, you may be able to comfort yourself by taking care of yourself in other ways.

Before you can successfully substitute anything, you must clearly understand the advantages you are receiving from the bad habit. This is the indicator of what you *really* need and the clue to where to find your substitutes. The replacement must offer you the same satisfaction as what it is replacing. Each person has a different profile of needs and means of satisfactions—but the mechanics of substitution are the same. It isn't *what* you substitute, it's whether or not you get the satisfaction you need.

Chart your needs. Diagnose your bad habits that answer those needs. Concoct your own new solutions. The preventive nostrums I am offering in this chapter come with a lot of instructions and blueprints, but you have to assemble them yourself.

Go to it, tiger. You tied the knots; you can untie them!

CHAPTER 17

How and How Not to Use Your Friends

When you need to broadcast and when you need encouragement, you need your friends. However, a word or two is in order about encouragement-getting. It is essential that you give out an air of confidence when you really feel confident. In other words, when you're up, you allow yourself to talk up about yourself. When you like something you've done, share your pleasure and satisfaction with those you love, false modesty be damned! Fake humility is no good. Sharing your good feelings about yourself conveys something positive to your friends and acquaintances which you should convey to them. Then, when you're feeling down, they return your positive feelings in the form of encouragement.

They don't know this is what has taken place. They are not aware of having negotiated a give-and-take contract with you, but this is what has happened. Because you conveyed a real sense of your own intrinsic worth (even if you only feel worthy once a year, on All Hallow's Eve), *your friends believe you are worthy.* When you feel insecure the other 364 days a year, they remember you are worthy and they put your downer in perspective for you. "Something has got to work out," they might assure you. Or, "Hang in there babe, you'll make it!" They are telling it to you when you most need to hear it from the outside. Remember, your unconscious is listening. But in order to get encouragement from your friends when you need it, you have to plant the crop yourself. (I hope to encourage you to plant it more than once a year.) Harvest will come at the right time.

When I was talking about broadcasting in chapter three, I mentioned picking good friends to air your troubles to. In addition to that qualification, you have to be very choosy about matching the right trouble to the right good friend. Selection of your audience (don't look askance at the word *audience*—I simply mean "who's listening") is of inestimable importance in terms of the response you will elicit.

Let's say, for example, that you have just finished writing the report you have been asked to deliver at an open meeting of your town's environmental protection committee. You are feeling all insecure and shaky because you haven't had any reactions to it as yet and you've worked so hard and so long on it—rewording, picking apart, trying to be clearer, and all the other things that require critical self-judgment—that by now you hate every damned word *and* yourself. However, *you know that* is par for the course, and you also know what you need—you need to hear an encouraging word, or what the shrinks call support.

In the old days, before you started figuring things out, you would simply have jumped on the nearest human form —friend or otherwise, whoever was passing by—and dumped. Something like, "I've just finished my report and I'd really value your opinion of it." Already you're in trouble. "Why?" you ask.

Because the person you jumped and dumped on:

1. wouldn't know a report from a resort
2. only reads doctor stories
3. is embroiled in a miserable love affair and hates the world
4. has just had his own report criticized to the high heavens
5. thinks she's God's gift to literary criticism
6. has always been covertly jealous of you since you won $500 in the New York State Lottery

7. has never forgiven you for being more attractive to a certain someone than she was (this could go back as far as age 14 and she's been waiting to get even ever since)
8. is in danger of being fired from his job and couldn't care less about anybody's report
9. has a sick stomach from a virus bug
10. was out on the town the night before, has a stinker of a headache, and was awakened by your phone call

I could go on with the list, but you get the point. You can't simply dump on the first person you encounter. And if you're honest, you wouldn't really value any ole body's reaction anyway. The selection technique should be as intricate as a Miss America Contest. We'll use your report again, although you could be asking encouragement on whether you'll get your promotion; does John still love you; is your new hairdo becoming; were you right in telling Alice what she could do with it; can you pass the course you registered for at the college, whatever. The principle of needing, asking for, and getting encouragement is the same.

It goes like this: First, you examine yourself (that's where you always start) and you figure out what responses you're looking for. Second, you calculate your margin of risk tolerance in case you don't get what you need despite your diabolical care and fiendish preselection techniques. Third, you take the answers to the first two questions—"I only want a quickie, 'that's wonderful' reaction" and "I can risk indifference at the 'un huh' level"—and you throw them into the hopper. Then you turn your beady, scheming eyes outward and survey the field. "Who's in town?" you ask yourself. Fourth, you look over the list of who's in town and you consider each in terms of the third-step answers. Immediately eliminate the first name because, as you well know, she considers herself a beautiful "out loud" reader and will be critical as hell of anyone else reading out loud. Of course, you're not asking her to judge your work on how you read it, but she *will*, she can't help herself. Save her for when you can give her a copy and ask her to read it to you—she'll be entranced. Since this is strictly an over-the-phone job, she's out. You'd be dead before you got through the first paragraph. Go through the rest of the list, sorting out your candidates *ahead of time*. Think about what each one's reaction is likely to be and why. Each time you eliminate one because you know you can't get the response you need, you should feel very smart for avoiding the downer that a lack of selection might have brought you.

As you go down the list, choose persons who are favorably disposed to you already. Don't pooh-pooh that suggestion as being automatic. I can't tell you how many times I used to set myself up for a drop-kick—before I learned that if you're looking for approval, don't look for it from someone who deep down hates your guts and wants nothing so much as to see you topple from the high horse they think you are astride.

Then consider several other questions about your candidates: Are they in the midst of problems or projects of their own which require their undivided attention? If so, save them for another day. Have you recently asked them for encouragement or approval about something else? Stay away for the moment if you want to keep from becoming a bore. You get to be a drag in a hurry if you turn to the same friend too often. The rule of thumb is that to ask a friend to take the time to give you a studied reaction once in a while is flattering; to ask too often is imposing.

Continuing the examination of personalities, you cross Bill off the list because, knowing Bill, the minute you utter the words, "I'd really value your opinion," he will don his black robe and sit on the Supreme Court. He takes it *seriously,* and he has this huge sense of responsibility which ends up forcing him to find fault in order to do justice to his high calling. The Bills of this world automatically translate the word *opinion* to mean "critical." *Avoid them like the plague!*

People don't usually realize these things about themselves and don't want to. In fact, if you ever confronted one of your friends with his reason for being disqualified, you'd probably end up in a knock-down drag-out fight. The main thing is, *you* have to know in order to side-step the dog do. (If you're tempted to challenge me on some of the foregoing description of the behavior of friends, let me remind you that nobody in the whole world is entirely free from ambivalence about anything! Your friends are entitled to their share of ambivalence about you and about what you do, just as you have and are entitled to ambivalence about them. Once you accept this, you will avoid an awful lot of disappointment and hurt—and, as I mentioned above, dog do.)

You have now winnowed out several candidates who meet all the criteria: they have not been used lately, they aren't competing with you in any tournament, they aren't swamped by their own problems at the moment, and they are intelligent and sensitive enough to be worth listening to. The final criterion is, "Who's home?"

It should be mentioned that *you* must be available for your friends when it's their turn to call and ask your opinion. (It might be interesting to run over the list of qualifications and see how you make out when you're approached.) Returning kindness and attention is one of the most important factors in a satisfying relationship and in not being a bore. It's unspoken, but very powerful. If you give this kind of sincere, supportive attention and interest, your friends will like giving it back. It makes for closeness and trust. It's sharing at its best. I love doing it with friends who love doing it with me. Don't you?

One word of caution on the subject of using your friends: be extra careful with friends whose profession it is to be an expert in the field about which you are consulting them. Don't ask them for casual reactions or casual encouragement. Asking shrink friends for advice to the lovelorn or your medical friends to diagnose your ulcer is like asking your friend who owns a candy store to keep you supplied with free lollipops. An emergency is one thing, but a casual request is another. So save your professional friends for help in a professional way, unless they want to *volunteer* help. That's a different story. You have not put them on the spot and you have shown proper respect. They'll appreciate that!

About encouragement or support—I do not mean unqualified compliments and kudos. I do not mean comments only on what is pleasing. Some of the best and most meaningful encouragement may very well include a great deal of fault-finding—*given in a positive framework*. Praise given grudgingly or fault found gleefully is equally worthless. The giving of criticism (which involves both praise and fault) is an art in itself. It requires taste, tact, love, and the ability to verbalize—but mainly it requires appreciation. I would like to make a distinction between *like* and *appreciate*. *Like* means something that only pleases your taste; *appreciate* means the ability to recognize and value the quality of what went into something, whether or not you like it. It is nice when people like what you do— your cooking, the way you've furnished your apartment, the way you dress, and so on. But liking or not liking is a totally personal reaction. Everyone is entitled to his or her own. You must bear this in mind when you're seeking encouragement and support, because it has to influence whom you ask and how you react. At the first step, when you decide what responses you're looking for, be sure to examine whether you want approval (someone to *like* what you're doing) or appreciation (someone to *understand* what you're doing).

If, when you've analyzed exactly what you're looking for, you discover that you just need to talk, then look for someone who will just listen.

Akin to broadcasting, the need to talk is perfectly respectable—some people think by talking. Much of the help you get from a shrink comes from sympathetic, understanding listening. Therefore, if you ascertain that it's talking you need (actually, it's *listening to* that you need), pick someone who can listen with understanding. Too often you just start talking to the first ear that calls up or the first mouth you have lunch with, or just anybody who happens to come along. *No good!* Why? Because there are standards. Being a good listener is no everyday virtue. It's an achievement. It's tough, one of the toughest things going. You think you pay shrinks for nothing? They spend years training to listen, and you sit there thinking it's easy for just anybody so it doesn't matter who you pick. Wrong. Wrong. Wrong.

Here are a few of the ordinary problems you run into if you don't select your listener:

Some would-be listeners are so busy preparing how to phrase their answer or advice that they don't hear a word you say.

Some people do not listen at all; they simply wait for you to stop talking so they can tell you *their* problem.

Some people automatically enter a contest with you the minute you open your mouth. They have several entries ready at all times to put up against anything you have to offer. It doesn't matter what happened to you—theirs was worse. When I said you should give and take with your friends, I didn't mean a free-for-all. You've got to find people who go along with taking turns.

Some people can't hear you even if they do listen, because the TV is always on or the kid is bawling.

Some people hear you, but you might as well be speaking Aramaic for all they understand. This is because their values are so totally different from yours that the whole time you're telling them the dire events that have befallen you, *they're thinking how lucky you are* to have had all that excitement! (Remember the old saying, If you spit on a whore, she'll say it's raining.) This is a matter of interpretation, and there are endless differences in the ways people react to the same stimuli.

Some people have the attention span of a gnat. If it's subtle, or the nuances require some background buildup, forget it—you'll never hold them. This is when you're spilling your guts to someone who keeps interrupting at crucial points with observations which are completely irrelevant. It's maddening. You're just coming to the climax of the story and they suddenly comment on what they saw on the street corner two days ago. The folks who do this are too nervous to listen to anything that lasts longer than twelve seconds. Don't tell them long jokes, either!

Some good friends are good listeners, but not when they have just landed after an eighteen-hour flight from Japan and have jet lag and need to retrieve their baggage from customs. Tired is no good because listening requires enormous energy. Good listening is as active as a Ping-Pong doubles match; it is a participatory sport . . . and, I do mean listening, not answering. Silent absorption is very hard work; paying complete attention is a real effort; so don't ask your good-listener friends to listen when they are exhausted any more than you would ask them to go on a nine-mile hike with you the minute they cross the finish line of the annual jogging marathon. Have a heart.

It's judgment I'm advocating, that's all. The thinking, figuring out, and selecting process is simply using judgment. Good judgment, like common sense, is a rare commodity. All my nostrums will boil down to common sense and judgment, and those two things, like simplicity itself, need to be worked for.

If you know your friends, you realize that some of them can listen to one thing but not another. Be choosy about whom you tell what to in terms of their preferences as well as yours. It'll pay off.

Finally, make your ratio of telling woes to having fun with any single friend roughly about one to twenty. Nobody loves a constant complainer.

There will be times when you cannot find *anyone* to talk to—three or four in the morning, for example. Then there is one ultimate friend you can always turn to—yourself.

I once talked eight hours straight to myself, and I got a lot out of it. But there's one catch. When you talk to yourself, *you've also got to listen*. Being a good listener to yourself requires the same kind of art as any other listening.

If you learn to be your own best listener, you'll discover that by the time you get around to talking to your friends, you'll already have gotten through the boring parts all alone.

Besides being good boredom prevention, I recommend talking to yourself *over* talking to anyone else because it is the best way to think about yourself and to discover who *you* are. Those are two of the most exciting things in the world!

CHAPTER 18

Helping Others

Helping others is one of those chicken-or-egg subjects. Do you have to help yourself first before you can help others? Or do you help others and thereby help yourself? I am inclined to say neither, or both, at the same time. The chicken carries the potential of the eggs, and the eggs carry the potential of the chicken. Each is always in the process of developing the other.

The chicken doesn't walk around and say, "I think I'll lay an egg today." Laying an egg is part of her nature. She walks around all right, but the egg inside her is developing —it's not something she decides to do or decides to withhold! Not everybody can lay eggs, of course. Roosters have their place, and may provide nourishment in the form of soup rather than omelet. Who's to say which is the greater gift to mankind?

Helping or giving to others comes out of a "can do" approach to living. The moment you think about helping someone else, you automatically assume a "can do" stance. And though you may not be aware of it at the moment, the "can do" attitude toward your own problems is also being strengthened and reinforced, so when the time comes for you to call on your own inner resources to help yourself, your "can do" will be ready, willing, and warmed up to serve you.

Helping others teaches you how to receive, accept, and use help for yourself. It affords you the opportunity to understand the donor's view and the donor's gain in giving, so that when your turn comes, you will be open and ready to receive the help that is offered. In this way, helping others is part of helping yourself and of being helped.

One of my dearest friends used to call me up and tell me her problems on a fairly regular basis, and I also told her mine. No matter what her problem was, I always felt obliged to come up with some idea for a solution. I felt frustrated if she didn't take my advice, and I felt terrible if she took it and it didn't help. One day she was in the middle of telling me her woes and I was in the middle of searching frantically for helpful suggestions when she suddenly said, "I don't really want you to give me any advice. Thank you, but I can figure things out for myself." Bewildered, I then asked her what she did want from me— why did she call me and tell me her problems.

"I just want you to be there," she said.

For the first time in our long relationship, I understood what I could give her and how. That slight exchange opened up a whole new era in our friendship, and it also taught me a great deal about the meaning of helping. Not long after that, I was telling her how down I was. "I feel like I've been out playing in traffic and I've been hit so often that all I can do is crawl over to the side of the road and lie there panting."

"I know," she replied. "It's not the cars, it's the trucks!"

That was one of the most understanding and comforting things anyone ever said to me. Not only did I laugh heartily, I really felt better.

When you are in the pits, one of the main problems is that you lose the confidence which would allow you to use your imagination and your flexibility. It seems virtually impossible to see how things could ever be any different (better). You cannot see any way to get out of the terrible hole you're in. Alternatives don't occur to you—you're so busy nursing your sore, painful psyche that you can't think! This is the moment when someone can come along and offer a few words of understanding (or just a consoling presence) and by so doing, change the balance. The smallest change can suffice to free you from the restrictive track of the maze you've been running.

An illustration of how you can be so intent on your problem that you can't think, is something that happened to me recently. I had parked my car outside a theater and gone to see a play. When I emerged, I was disturbed but not surprised to find that a taxicab had double-parked, blocking my car totally. This is not too unusual in New York City, so I did all the routine things one does in this situation. I tried the taxi doors (all locked), I blew my horn insistently (no response, but then who notices in Greenwich Village?). Then I went to the nearest open delicatessen, figuring that the cabbie was buying his supper, and inquired loudly to one and all as to whether anyone had a yellow cab double-parked outside.

All to no avail.

Time passed, and I grew increasingly irritated.

A man came over to my car window, which was closed because it was a bitterly cold night, and seemed to be asking for a handout—also typical of New York City, and not what I was in the mood for at that moment. I waved him away, convinced that he was up to no good.

More time passed, and still no cabbie.

By this time, I had gotten in and out of my car, trying the taxi doors and stalking the area at least a half-dozen times, blowing my horn, snorting and pawing the ground.

Finally, I called the police. They said they would dispatch a patrol car.

While I was waiting (I had to remain outside in the cold to hail the police when they arrived), a young woman who had been inside the delicatessen approached me and said she thought she had seen the driver of the cab go into the restaurant across the street.

I dashed across the street to the restaurant and breathlessly announced my dilemma to the cashier (I refrained from shouting it aloud this time, although I was tempted to do so). The cashier felt that he was not harboring my cabbie, so I departed once again into the frigid air.

The taxi door handles remained adamant, so I called the police a second time. After two dozen rings, they answered the phone. The entire story had to be repeated, since it seemed to be brand new to the woman on the other end of the phone. She would, she assured me, send a patrol car.

Back to the street I went, half-expecting a siren and flashing lights to greet me within thirty-four seconds.

Nothing.

Frozen and frustrated, I got back into my car for a five-minute injection of warmth from the heater. At this point, the same man who had approached my car window before, could be seen making a phone call from a nearby booth. Then he went over to the cab and tried the handle himself.

A light went on in my head, and I got out of my car. He said to me (quite soberly, I must admit with chagrin) that it was his cab and that he had been trying to tell me that when I had waved him away. He told me that he had called his office and was waiting for help to arrive. The problem had to do with the fact that this was not his regular cab. The keys he had been given did not fit the door, so when he had locked it to go into the deli, he had not been able, upon his return, to reopen the door. (He offered this explanation in a rather huffy manner, since he was irritated, and rightly so, by my having cold-shouldered him before, and by my arrogant assumption that the problem lay with his ineptitude.)

After forty-five more minutes had passed and we were both standing in the freezing cold waiting for either his company to send help or the police to arrive—neither of us cared which—we had developed a sense of camaraderie about the whole matter. We exchanged ideas about hangers and other means of possibly opening the door.

Then he turned to me and suggested, "Why don't you go into the restaurant across the street and ask them to move their truck?"

I was dumbfounded. The restaurant's truck was parked directly in front of me, and the name was clearly emblazoned in large letters on the rear door. It had been visible the entire time! In fact, I had noted the name because I had gone into the same restaurant looking for my new friend, the cabbie.

I took his advice, and within two minutes I was free and clear. I could have done this an hour and a half earlier and been free and clear. I was so blocked by how I was feeling—frustrated and irritated and cold—that I had not been thinking! I had not recognized and dealt with the real problem, which was how to get out of the spot I was in, and had gotten tangled up in where is the cabbie who is blocking me.

To finish my tale, my friend and I parted on very good terms. He had indeed helped me. Not only did he offer me advice and an alternative I couldn't see for myself, but he helped me learn a very important object lesson: When you are completely caught up by how miserable you are feeling, your ability to help yourself by thinking about your problem is diminished. You become trapped by the maze of your own feelings.

Unless you can think calmly about what your real problem is and tackle that, you are destined to go around and around repeating the same fruitless pattern and being frustrated at the same unyielding junctures. You must learn to relinquish your preoccupation with how awful the situation is, and think *only* about what you can do to alter it.

There are always alternatives.

You must free yourself from the rigid, inflexible, self-defeating rut you get into when you feel depressed and really look at your problem. The minute you do so, you will begin to perceive possible solutions. And you will feel better!

If you are offering help to someone else, try, like my friend the cabbie, to address the real problem rather than lecturing on the blockage. When you or someone you are trying to help is depressed, you need to *find* an opening, not *make* one. Too hard a push can cause you or your depressed friend to flare up in anger and resist the help you might otherwise benefit from.

Helping is not necessarily doing.
Helping can be just being there.
Helping can be understanding.

Being there and understanding can make the difference when someone is in a bad downer. A word, a willing ear, a comforting touch, or a pair of arms wrapped around someone can make the difference and turn the balance toward feeling better.

Give and let give.

CHAPTER 19

The Honeymoon Principle

The honeymoon principle is based on a universal trait recognizable in human beings: we are all crazy about something new. Watch children play with their new Christmas toys like mad for a few days and then go back to their old favorites; watch Dad polish the new car, and, for the first month, wipe off every speck of dust; watch Suzy wear a different outfit for her new beau for the first six dates; watch Joe send flowers after the first time and then settle into a comfortable arrangement. Watch yourself with a new restaurant, a new recipe, a new hobby, new furniture, a new outfit, new games, or a new president. Watch other people when you first begin a new job or meet new people—all these are examples of the honeymoon principle at work. The *honeymoon* is literally the "sweet month"—it gets its name from the first month newlywed couples spend together when they are first enjoying the newness of their relationship. It is a time of suspended criticality; a time of going more than halfway to meet and/or accommodate; a time of finding pleasure rather than flaws.

The newness of anything commands your attention in a very special and very pleasurable way. I think this tendency is related to the animal curiosity which impels us to explore new things because it is so interesting to do so. Exploration leads to discovery as a side effect, which is nature's way to get us to adapt and improve our lot. But, as in all her endeavors, Mother Nature is very sneaky and tricky about her real motives. She manipulates us outrageously, and we love it!

The best story I know to illustrate just what a fraud Mother Nature really is and to what lengths she will go to manipulate her creatures is the case of certain genus of orchid. If memory serves, it's called *Orchis oxybellum,* or close to it. For years, no one could figure out how this elegant flower managed to attract the gentlemen flies who transported the pollen from one flower to the other. There was no discernible lure, no nectar, no tantalizingly sweet scent. Yet the gentlemen flies made their rounds faithfully and the orchid flourished.

Finally, the secret was discovered. There *was* a scent. But it was not the kind of scent exuded by other flowers. Oh no! This delicate beauty cleverly exuded the exact scent of the *lady fly.* How's that for knowing how to get what you want? And to top it off, inside the orchid, at the precise place where Mother Nature wanted the pollen to be deposited, she had shaped the flower in a perfect replication of the sexual organs of the lady fly! Need I tell you what the old boy does to the orchid, thinking it's the new girl on the block? In the process, the orchid has the necessary pollen distributed plentifully where it does the most good. If that isn't a fraud, I don't know what is. So whenever I hear grand stories about how "innocent" and "honest" and "true" Mother Nature is, I have to smile. Mother Nature is the arch contriver of all times!

Her contrivances, however, are not arbitrary. The fraudulent equipment with which she often endows her creatures helps them survive. And for those who say she isn't fair, I say at least she's fairly evenhanded. (I may not have a fierce red throat that will scare the daylights out of anything that contemplates going for my jugular, but I *do* have an opposable thumb and the ability to imagine things before they happen—both of which are nifty items if you learn how to use them.)

The honeymoon principle is one of Mother Nature's finer frauds. My definition of sexual attraction is "Nature's way of getting two people to stay together long enough to fall in love." Most people think that the sexual attraction part *is* falling in love; I think it's the replica which gets us to do what she wants! I don't knock it, however, because it has its compensations and it serves it purpose.

What has all this honeymoon and fraud business to do with depression? *Anything* is likely to have some beneficial effect when you first try it. Something new and different will distract you because it is new and different. A new idea holds promise and brings relief because you have hope that it will. When you begin to try the nostrums in this book, capitalize on the honeymoon principle—but don't run any single nostrum into the ground. If you do, it may stop working for you and leave you feeling let down and "had" again. You must understand the honeymoon principle and make it work for you.

The whole arsenal of various nostrums—alternating, switching, developing variations and wrinkles of your own —all these changes of pace or points of view will help you keep the newness and the freshness intact while you're learning to fall in love with feeling good about yourself.

Fighting depression is war. And in war, there are many weapons in the arsenal. Depending on the terrain, the objective, the resistance, your resources at a given moment, you have to plan your tactics and employ your arsenal with discretion. You must marshal your forces and attack the enemy like the Furies. Plan! Use strategy! Deploy your troops! Keep your armory well stocked. Whether you're involved in light skirmishes or epic battles, you are your own general, and you have to muster your forces and resources to win the battles and the war. The honeymoon principle is one of the strategies you can make work for you. Their very newness will make you feel better when you first begin to try some of the nostrums. But go beyond that—take yourself on a honeymoon.

For one month, beginning today, spend a honeymoon with yourself.

If you think about it for a moment, you will realize that you are married to yourself, for better or worse, in sickness, in health—and *forever*. Why not work to make it a happy marriage?

Happy marriages are characterized by love and consideration, understanding, affection, companionship, shared fun and shared pain, trust, dependability, and a mutual striving toward goals. In your marriage to yourself, these same things apply. Regard your relationship with yourself exactly this way, and make up your mind that you are going to make it a good one. (If you've got a mate already, you'll be a bigamist for a month!)

Treat yourself as if you are in love with you and want nothing so much in the world as to make you happy.

Bring yourself flowers.

Take yourself out.

Talk to yourself and listen rapturously.

Be understanding and interested in getting to know you—every wart, every hair on your beautiful head.

Groom yourself carefully and dress up for you.

Make love to yourself.

Fix breakfast in bed for yourself.

Stroke yourself and admire yourself.

Look for your virtues and praise them aloud to you.

Make plans and discuss your dreams with yourself.

Overlook your foibles and minimize your faults.

Do everything you can to make you happy.

Don't criticize *anything* you do.

Revel in how wonderful you are and how lucky you are to have you.

Split a bottle of champagne with yourself.

Dance with yourself.

Listen to music together.

Do all these things and more for one month. My feeling is that you will grow to love yourself better than you ever have before. Loving yourself better is the beginning of being happy with yourself for the rest of your life.

The nice thing is that not only is bigamy permitted, but once you fall in love with *you*, you'll end up falling in love with all kinds of people, places, and things, in all kinds of ways.

If you can make you happy, you can make someone else happy.

Here's looking at you—together.

CHAPTER 20

Loneliness—How It Relates and How You Only Think It Relates

I know a very bright, gifted, resourceful, successful, attractive woman who has a severe problem with habitual depression. As far as I can discern, it seems to stem almost entirely from what she perceives as loneliness.

In addition to all the positive attributes I just listed, she dresses well, is in good health, is cultivated, has numerous friends, and is very much in demand socially. She has her own work, which she finds gratifying and richly rewarding on all levels. Of the four pillars that support happiness, I would count her as having three. She has everything in the world you can think of to make a person happy *except a mate*.

The missing pillar, of course, is love. But that is not what is really making her so miserable. There is one thing wrong with this lucky woman that spoils everything else she has in life—she has not yet learned how to make herself happy.

She blames her chronic and unrelenting state of depression on loneliness. When she goes out and enjoys herself of an evening, she becomes depressed when she returns home because she's home alone. If she brings her date home with her, she's depressed the next day when he leaves because it was an "empty" experience and she feels more alone than ever.

She was alone the whole time, of course. We're alone the whole time.

We spend our lives with ourselves—and share some of it in the company of others. But the best any of us can manage is to sit, walk, stand, or lie *next to* someone else. The single and only instance when it might be argued that two human beings are truly united is when one of them is in the other's womb. I will not explore the symbolic overtones of that statement in relation to sex, but I'm sure you will make the connection.

I grant you that it is very scary walking around on this planet all by yourself. It was very scary leaving the womb. And it is very scary leaving this life. All these things are scary because we have a terrific imagination and project every conceivable and inconceivable threat and horror onto the unknown.

On the other hand, those who have experienced and survived the chill of the unknown have discovered that it wasn't too bad—along with the chill there was a certain thrill. This is what occurs when children begin to venture outside, preferring the world's strangeness and challenge to the safety of home. As I said earlier, we have a taste for adventure and risk and discovery or we wouldn't still be here as a species.

My idea of a good balance is to go out venturing all day (on whatever frontier) and then come home at night to your cave, throw whatever you've captured on the floor, and say to the one you might be sharing it with, "Ugh, this one put up a helluva struggle, but I loved every minute of it."

Now if you don't have someone to share your spoils and show your victory off to, you may not enjoy them quite so much as if you had—but the difference is between more and less enjoyment, not enjoyment versus depression!

If you enjoy your spoils all by yourself (as well you can and should), it will soon occur to your tousled head that it would be even more fun to show off what you captured before you devour it. It might be even more fun to share some of it and maybe trade some of yours for some of someone else's. (This idea of sharing has primeval roots, but can be seen in contemporary life in the way people order at Chinese restaurants.)

Getting back to this person who has everything except a mate. Her trouble is that she has everything except a mate. Because she has everything else, she has focused on the one thing she lacks and has located it as her source of unhappiness. I think that this woman is suffering from the opposite of what I was discussing in chapter sixteen—she not only has enough, she has too much!

Actually, she has too few goals left, too few desires. As she acquired the conventional rewards, she failed to develop new goals and desires. This woman, like every other human being, needs dreams and challenges to enrich and enliven her existence. As her store of dreams, goals, and wants was fulfilled, she neglected to replenish it. And now she has to enlarge the one thing she hasn't got to fill up all the spaces and holes that are still there for her, just as if she had a whole larderful of wants. Here again, you have the opposite situation, where there is no satisfaction because enough is too much.

The solution to her problem, it seems to me, would not be to find a mate (who might or might not make her happy) but to find a couple of hundred *other* things to want. To have numerous other desirable goals and ambitions and dreams. To expand her horizons and spread her wings. To increase her investments. To explore new areas. To care about multifarious outcomes. To put out for various endeavors and causes and cases and friends.

Ironically, it may very well be that she is unable to find a mate who suits her because no one individual can meet all those needs which she has so diligently rolled up into a single place. If she ever finds a person who seems suitable, she will be likely to drown him as she pours all that need into the one basket.

This woman is practicing a form of self-deception which distracts her from her real problems and gives her a handy excuse for her unhappiness. It seems to me that she is clinging to a childhood dream of love and security, and refuses to let go in order to learn to make herself happy. What's more, I believe she knows she's doing this, but she does not want to face the responsibility of making her own life complete and satisfying.

* * *

Why do we continue to cling to old patterns that keep us miserable? In this instance, I can see two major reasons. The first is a form of self-punishment that attends loneliness—you feel you don't deserve *not* to feel lonely. (Those who are not alone nevertheless feel they don't deserve to be happy.) Very often this "undeservingness," which can both prevent a person from trying to achieve and prevent enjoyment of what has been achieved, is a means of perpetuating the feelings of childhood when there was a deprivation of love—and, as a result, the child learned to feel unworthy. (In the clear reasoning of the child, if one is worthy of being loved, surely one will be loved.) It is only much later, if ever, that the unloved child begins to comprehend that parents are also human beings who may have hangups and who may not be able to *give* love.

If you don't believe you deserve happiness, you're going to find a rich assortment of ways to bat down the opportunities for having it. Unless you can break out of this perpetual self-punishing and self-withholding pattern, you can spend the rest of your life depriving yourself of friendship, closeness, love, help, intimacy, happiness, and joy *to prove that your parents were right all along.*

So much for the number-one reason for loneliness. The number-two reason is fear. Fear of the unknown. Fear of change. Fear of failure. Fear of inadequacy. Fear of being tested. Fear of not measuring up. Fear, too, can be a habit. Originally intended as a safeguard to keep us alert to danger, fear can be abused and corrupted into a habitual, unthinking response to newness. It can replace curiosity, which leads us toward new experience; obliterate the Honeymoon Principle, which allows us to delight in the new; and cause us to withdraw from and shun the unfamiliar. Like anger, fear has to be used properly, not stifled or stomped on. There's an old saying that goes, I'm not afraid, I'm just cautious. The truth in this is that you are afraid, but that fear is serving the purpose for which it was intended—namely *to make you cautious.*

Perhaps a handy way to differentiate between wholesome fear and the fear that binds you is that wholesome fear is usually directed toward something specific. Unwholesome fear, confining and restricting and stifling fear, is undirected, unspecific, generalized, and abstract. It acts like a kind of matrix in which more and more activity becomes embedded.

Sometimes a person seems to develop a fear suddenly in an area where he or she had previously felt confident. When this happens, very often it is attributable not to the generalized, abstract kind of reaction I have been talking about, but to the body's issuance of a cautionary message —that message might read: "You're tired, your energy level is not up to par, therefore your reflexes are going to be a little bit off." In other words, on some very subtle level, your body knows you are not at your best and that your performance is bound to suffer because of it—so you are being given a warning in the form of fear. This is a message which you should learn to heed. No one is always at her or his best, and if you recognize those times when you're not, you can adjust for a slightly lower performance level. By becoming aware of your body's warnings and learning to trust them, you turn nonspecific fear into specific fear. In this way, you achieve two things: you allow yourself leeway in performance without being critical, and you prevent the spreading of fear that would occur if it remained nonspecific. You understand what is happening and therefore it becomes known and unthreatening.

Of course, specific fear has to be dealt with and mastered. (You may recall my story about the audition I had to take.) Specific fear has the element of thrill that I mentioned earlier—it can be exciting, stimulating, and capable of adding an edge to performance. In Italy, there is an opera house which, from the singers' point of view on stage, looks like the open maw of a huge wolf. Before a performance, the singers say to each other, *"In bocca di lupo!"* which means, "Into the mouth of the wolf!"

In other words, that's where you've got to throw it— right in his teeth! It takes courage to face the maw of whatever you're up against. It takes courage to live and to learn to be happy. And you are never truly alive unless you do so.

One of my favorite stories my father used to tell me when I was a child (he had a number of stories which all revolved around overcoming enemies in the form of beasts) was about a fight he had with a wolf. In my father's story, he was fighting fiercely with the wolf, and I was following every detail with excitement and breathless anticipation of the next development. At the climax of the story, which always ended the same way, my father concluded with, "And then I reached into his throat, caught hold of the end of his tail, and pulled him inside out!"

Right then and there, my father gave me one of the best nostrums in the world for combating depression or assorted other troubles. Because, as I was discussing in chapter two, using the opposite of something (pulling it inside out) can be very effective as a means of counteracting it.

In the case in point: if you are depressed because you're lonely, instead of running around madly seeking the company of others, do the opposite. Cultivate your own company! Develop pleasure and satisfaction in being alone. Revel in and relish being with you and doing things with yourself. There are many ways to enjoy your own company. In fact, some occupations are so absorbing that the presence of someone else is a distraction. While reading, for example, or serious stamp collecting, or numerous other creative endeavors, it is inordinately difficult to think when you are with someone. I do not mean the ordinary run-of-the-mill kind of thinking, such as "Where did I put the keys to the car?" or "What time do I have to put the roast in the oven?" I mean creative, problem-solving, real figuring-out thinking, which I have been advocating all along. You have to do this by yourself; and if you let yourself, it will help you learn to enjoy the pleasures of your own mind.

In addition to the list of things I suggested in chapter nineteen which you should do for yourself and with yourself on your honeymoon with you, there are many, many ways to enjoy your own company and be creative. Since each of us has different tastes, let my list serve as a point of departure for the one you make up for yourself. Here are some suggestions:

    reading
    stamp collecting
    coin collecting
    any kind of collecting

craft work: sewing, needlework, woodwork, pottery, jewelry
gardening
raising plants
listening to and watching TV
taking courses
going to museums
going to zoos, parks, movies, plays, concerts
cooking
shopping
walking
bicycling, skating, horseback riding, swimming, fishing
listening to music
traveling
attending lectures
home repair and decorating

The list could go on and on, and if you object to at least half of it on the ground that they are better done *with* someone, let me say that I agree—some of them could— but they need not, and if you go ahead and start doing them alone, you'll probably find congenial people to do them with along the way.

Aloneness is not loneliness. I am not overlooking the need we all have for the company and stimulation provided by contact with others. Most of us need that contact (religious hermits excepted—but they have established a connection with the universe within their own minds and their communication is on a different plane). Aloneness, when tempered by, alternated with, and contrasted to companionship, is not only nourishing to the spirit, it is essential to a certain kind of personal growth and development.

Thinking creatively is not reserved for artists or scientists, as I have said before. Many of the most successful people in business think creatively about business. I have long been of the opinion that business, in fact, is an American art form. If you cross-compare, you'll find the same elements: goal-oriented planning; keeping in mind how the parts relate to the whole; making decisions about techniques, and time factors, and best use of resources.

And, like the business person, the artist must also think about promotion and marketing.

Creativity comes into every activity you set your mind and hand to. Creativity is problem solving: watch an infant turn a stoppered bottle around and around, trying to figure out a way to get the stopper out; watch your husband reading the directions for the operation of the fancy new lawn mower; watch your son studying football formations; watch your daughter planning which courses to take next semester; watch your mother and father figuring out a new budget for their fixed income; watch yourself as you go through each day having to meet countless problems and challenges—each uses creative faculties constantly.

Ours is a creative-thinking species. And, returning full circle to my original point, ninety-nine times out of one hundred, creative thinking must be done solo. This is why so many artists have, on one hand, a hard time securing enough solitude to work in, and on the other, enough contact and stimulation.

If you suffer from what you have labeled loneliness, it may appall you to hear that May Sarton wrote an entire book called *Solitude*, and what that condition can offer. Also, Carolyn Wyeth has stated unequivocally that she must be alone in order to paint. Almost every creative person has to come to terms with the dual need for solitude and contact in one way or another. Sometimes chance manages it for the artist (I wonder how many books have been written in jail). But most often, the creative person must find a way to secure aloneness in order to work.

One of the happiest arrangements I can think of existed between Simone de Beauvoir and Jean-Paul Sartre in their early life together. Each spent the day alone, working in separate areas of the house they shared. In the evening, they came together to share a meal and read to each other from what they had written during the day. I, for one, cannot think of anything that sounds more idyllic than two people who respect each other living individual lives of integrity and sharing them side by side.

As human beings, we have been endowed with extraordinary sensory equipment as a means of protection and survival. Stimuli bombard us incessantly from all sides. Even though our stimuli-processing equipment is fantastically efficient, even though our receptors feed information to our brains at lightning speeds—so fast that we think we are receiving many stimuli simultaneously—we are, in fact, receiving them one at a time and processing them singly.

Here is what Arthur Koestler says about "stimuli processing" in *The Act of Creation:*

> We constantly scan the field with, mostly unconscious, movements of the eye, to bring the blurred periphery into the narrow beam of focal vision—pinpointed at the fovea, the tiny spot at the centre of the retina which alone conveys true and distinct sight.
>
> In 1960, experiments at McGill University led to the rather surprising discovery that the unconscious movements of the eye are not merely aids to clearer vision, but a sine qua non of vision.
>
> When the subject's gaze remained really fixed on a stationary object (by means of a mechanical device) his vision went haywire, the image of the object disintegrated and disappeared—then reappeared after a while but in distorted shape or in fragments. Static vision does not exist; there is no seeing without exploring. . . .

We pay attention alternately. We flit from one perception to another at incredibly rapid speeds. We are not gifted for concentration by natural endowment or disposition. We must *learn* to concentrate. Even our reactions to emotional and psychological stimuli consistently bounce back and forth between negative and positive feelings. Someone once told me, "There is no such thing as a pure motive." And the more years I spend thinking about that, the more true it seems. We are just too complex to have pure reactions about anything. This is one of the things we plague ourselves with for not having—as if there is something the matter with us because we vacillate. Vacillating, alternating, feeling dualities and ambivalences is *normal*. We act on convictions because of the weightiest or most prevalent feeling—but never on a single, uncontaminated, *pure* feeling.

It is not easy to shut out the ceaseless bombardment of incoming sensations, which is why concentration is difficult. But, as I said before, it can be learned. It must be learned if you are to think creatively about your problems and your life.

And you can learn to be happy. It is natural and instinctive for you to be so. Create your happiness with your innate mental ability to control your thoughts—to direct them, to use them toward positive goals.

All this takes enormous powers of concentration. So use your time alone to teach yourself the art of being happy.

The paradox is that when you learn to enjoy being alone because you have tapped into the riches of your own mind, you will be sought after by others as you never have been before.

CHAPTER 21

Ways to Bolster Your Ego or When You Feel Like a Piece of Garbage, How to Climb on Top of the Heap

Many of the nostrums that have come under different headings earlier in this book are also ways to bolster your ego: comparison, for one; the encouragement you receive from friends; the opening of "praise accounts"; the development of a "can do" self-image through helping others; the honeymoon you should take with yourself; and so on. But since a puny ego is one of the main preconditions for depression, it is worth devoting a chapter to all by itself.

One thing that infuriates me is the way some people put down other people for having an ego. "You certainly do have an ego!" they may say, with that tone of voice which indicates disapprobation. Of course you have an ego; you need to have an ego. It takes an ego to comb your hair! It takes an ego to open up your front door and go outside to greet the world. It takes an ego to get married and have children. It takes an ego to get out of an unhappy relationship. People with little or no ego are in bad trouble. And yet, all too often the person who believes in himself or herself enough to try to accomplish something is accused of being an egotist (or egoist; I don't know what the difference is and I doubt seriously that most of the people who fling the term at you know either).

It seems to me that this accusation tends to come from those who have not dared to attempt very much themselves, or who have not liked the result of what they have attempted. By putting the person down who has attempted and who is pleased by the results of the attempts, they get themselves off the hook.

Let me urge you to say, "Thank God I do have an ego." I can issue you a gilt-edged guarantee that you will not be thoughtless, selfish, unfeeling, or insensitive to others because you have an ego. On the contrary, a healthy ego is one of the best assurances that you will be concerned and caring about others.

All the foregoing is to make sure that you are convinced that bolstering your ego is a good thing to do. In dealing with someone else's notions about what you should not feel in this area, let me recommend one of the best answers for dealing with the "put-down of your ego" point of view. Actually, the answer is a gesture—the *shrug*. (I hope it will become the newest dance step rage).

The *Shrug* is a sidestep which enables you to glide smoothly and beautifully across the floor and out of the way of criticism. It circumvents words of retort, which would only be fodder for your critic to chew up and spit back at you, and it conveys your indifference in letting the other fellow think what he wants, but you don't have to agree. The shrug indicates clearly that you do not feel a sense of responsibility for what someone else says or thinks or does. You aren't trying to convince people that they're wrong, and you neither have to go along with their view or find fault with them for having it. Try it! By shrugging, you satisfy your ego in not concurring just to avoid disagreement or gain approval, and you sidestep what would be a futile discussion.

Your ego feelings rest to a large extent on what might be called the recognition factor. No matter how meager your circumstances, how long a run of bad luck you've been on, how modestly nature has endowed you, *you are unique* and should be recognized as being the unique person you are. Nobody wants to walk around like a cipher, and being a statistic is even worse. You are a human being, the only one like you that ever will walk on the face of this earth. One of the ideas that keeps my jaw hanging loose in marvel is that each and every one of us is absolutely unique—and yet so much like our fellow creatures at the same time. This seeming paradox positions every living thing in a most fascinating way. We're what might be described as Janus-faced in the ego department: proud of being oneself and only oneself (looking in one direction), and humble about being only one among so many (looking in the other direction). In other words, you're one of a kind at the same time that you're one of your kind.

You want the world to recognize the first half of that statement, and I want you to recognize the second half. It's a kind of double recognition. Here is a story that illustrates double recognition. I was walking along the street about twenty-five paces behind a bum. Parked at the curb a few feet ahead of both of us was a brand-new Cadillac. An extremely well-dressed man was loading the trunk with a set of expensive golf clubs when the bum approached him for a handout. The well-dressed man turned to the bum, smiled warmly, and responded, "Why, I was just going to ask you!"

A broad grin of pleasure spread across the bum's face. He continued down the street without another word, chuckling to himself, full of good humor and delight. The bum knew that the well-dressed man was gently pulling his leg, but it made him feel like a million dollars. It made me feel like a million dollars just to see it take place.

With a gesture, that gentleman did more for the bum than any amount of money he might have offered. I have admired and respected the gentleman golfer from that day to this. Everybody recognized everybody—both the "one of a kind" and the "one of your kind" aspects. The bum felt good about himself. The golfer felt good about himself. I felt good about both of them and about myself. This was a conjunction of happy and satisfying human relations. Nobody ever improved by feeling bad about themselves. First you've got to believe that there are at least *some* good things about you. Then you can try to make them better. Finally, you can bring yourself up to your best level and carry it over to other areas.

Start at a place where you feel you have the most solid

ground beneath you—a positive and good foundation. Then build upward and outward from what is solid, one stone at a time. One stone supports and fortifies the next. You don't build an arch out of one stone, however, so building your ego, like building an arch, takes some doing. But once you get it built, it's an architectural marvel and it can carry quite a load.

Getting down to cases (or ego-building blocks), I suggest you go about constructing your arch as follows: get out the pen or pencil again and start to write down a list of things you do well or are good at. No matter how low you feel, you can come up with good things that it is possible for you to like about yourself. No one is going to see this list except you, so now's your chance to admit that you've always thought you have beautifully expressive eyes, or well-formed hands, or a sonorous speaking voice, or a nicely shaped forehead. Or maybe you do the tango splendidly but never have the chance. *Write them down*— and try not to stop until you have twenty-five items. Large or small, obvious or subtle, it doesn't matter. I don't even care if you record the fact that you wear your shoes down evenly. If you really put your mind to it, you can do it. Now label this A. You are the only judge of what gets put on this list—and it must consist of what pleases you. Whether anybody else thinks your selections are valid doesn't matter.

I want you to add at least three to five *more* items to this list every day—maybe you're proud of the fact that you sleep "neat," for example (the covers are not all messed up every morning). Write it on the list if you are pleased about it. You must continue to add three to five new things every day for three weeks. I promise you that if you do this, before the three weeks are up, you will begin to notice an increase in the strength of your good feelings about yourself. You must be sincere, however, and faithful. Don't let a day go by that you don't find good things about yourself.

At the end of three weeks (or twenty-one days, whichever comes first), you will be ready to start list B. List B must not be undertaken until *after* you have completed the three weeks of making List A.

List B is very simple. Just write down one dozen things you have done in your life that gave you a feeling of satisfaction or accomplishment. If you read all of James Joyce's *Ulysses* and you feel that was an accomplishment (I do), then write that on List B. If you graduated from high school or college and you feel that meant something, write it down! If you've learned how to type or ride a bicycle or say, "May I have the bill?" in French, put that on. Then add one more thing to List B every day for three *more* weeks. Got it?

At the end of the second three weeks, look over all of List B and List A.

Then you will be ready to assay List C.

One word of caution: do not attempt to make List B before List A, or to make either of them in less than three weeks. If you do, my guarantee of a strong ego arch does not hold.

List C is eight things you want to accomplish but have been afraid you could not. These may be things you have already been working toward or they may include things you have not heretofore even let yourself think about. Perhaps it's your lifelong wish that you could learn to play the piano or go back to school; maybe it's your buried dream of having your own business. Do not worry about how you will manage to do them. That will come later, after you decide what you really want first. (This is when you will begin walking around your boulder again, because you will discover that your boulder is also anything you want to budge.)

Add one new thing you want to do every day for the next three weeks.

I have just given you the ABCs of how to climb on top of the heap, and you don't have to be feeling like a piece of garbage to do it! If you spend the next nine weeks making your lists, you'll end up on top of the heap and on top of the world, because if you strain your brain for nine whole weeks thinking of all these positive, likeable, pleasurable, good, desirable things, you're going to spend nine weeks thinking about *good* things about you instead of your dumps. And you're going to get out of making yourself a garbage heap or letting anyone else give you a shove in that direction.

Good thoughts and good feelings reinforce each other. It's as simple as that. The better you feel about you, the better you will function and the better you will do things which will make you feel better about yourself. This is not a secret; it's as old as the hills. I didn't invent it, but I did reinvent it on my own hide—which is what I am asking you to do. There is no such thing as abstract wisdom or good sense. It doesn't exist until it is invented on *your* hide. Then and then only does advice become wisdom or good sense—when you take it and make it work for you. You are the only one who can. Nothing will work for you unless you work for it.

That's going to take some determination and some discipline. If you're too lazy to be bothered, then I hope you've had a few smiles reading this book, because that's all you're going to get out of it and I don't want it to be a total waste. But if you make the determination and exercise the discipline, *you can overcome depression.* I know. I've done it.

I've tried the nostrums in this book and had them work for me. I have, in a sense, been the laboratory for testing the recipes I'm offering you in this book. I also know that discipline can be learned. It can be practiced, like playing scales or throwing darts. Assign yourself certain small things to carry out every day, and do them come hell or high water. As a matter of fact, you're already practicing a number of forms of self-discipline: you brush your teeth every day, you get dressed, you wash your face, you comb your hair. So all you have to concern yourself with is adding one or two new items to your life—things that will be good for you or will make you feel good about yourself —and do them religiously.

In practicing your discipline exercises, regularity and faithfulness are more important than the length of time you spend. Five minutes worth of physical exercises every day, or one phone call to a friend or acquaintance daily (if you have trouble communicating), polishing your shoes once a week, reading ten pages of a book every day—*what you choose to discipline yourself with doesn't matter.* This is discipline for the sake of discipline—although as an added dividend, you are doing something good for you.

The art of self-discipline, once it is learned, can be

243

applied to any area of your life. But you have to start practicing it somewhere, sometime. I want to call your attention to one fact about determination. It is the fuel that runs your engine, the force of will and mental energy that you must expend—but it cannot be successfully expended at full, open throttle every minute, all the time. Determination must be expended in a technique of grip-release. Picture yourself sliding down a greased flagpole. Most of the time you are gripping like crazy to keep from plummeting to the bottom. But some of the time you have to ease up on the pressure (release), because you cannot sustain tension unremittingly. There has to be some relaxation in order for you to exert renewed force. If you understand this, you will know that you keep control even when you let up—and that you are not going around determined and disciplined every second of the day.

The shrug has its place as a gesture. And I want you to think about the fact that in addition to the many *words* I've talked about that characterize depression, there are also *gestures* that characterize it.

These gestures, among countless others that express inner feelings, have come to be know as body language. Very often, people who are depressed have a characteristic droopy look or hangdog expression. Their stance is a slouch, and the corners of their mouths turn downward. They tend to walk with eyes cast down, looking at the ground. But besides these out-and-out physical manifestations of depression, there are a number of mental attitudes which have taken on physical names to characterize the typical responses of the depressed person. They are "mental gestures" in a way, and though they are more subtle and harder to spot than the purely external ones, it is worthwhile observing yourself to see which ones you may make.

Your gestures may not be the same as mine, so you'll have to watch yourself pretty hard to spot what you typically do to express your depression. You might, for example, do the mental *wallow*—or perhaps, in your mind, you shake your head from side to side, continually indicating *no.* Your typical mental response could be the *dodge* or the *duck* or the *shirk* or the *cheekturn.* Pick out what you do habitually to express your depression through mental gestures, then replace whatever it is with the *handshake*. When you complete your five minutes of exercises or your phone call or your ten pages of reading, do the *handshake* with yourself. If you have several gestures that need replacement, also add the *pat on the back* to your repertoire and learn to do the "tuck your thumbs under your armpits" routine. Just be sure to include a self-congratulatory gesture after each achievement of discipline every day until your new gestures become second nature, just as I am sure your old self-denigrating gestures are now. At first, make your new mental gesture outwardly. Then, when you begin to feel that there is something missing if you do not make this self-congratulatory gesture, you are ready to turn it inward and let it become mental (Not everyone would understand if you went around shaking your own hand in public, or patting yourself on the back.)

First, of course, you have to catch onto your own gestures of denial and self-condemnation, and that isn't easy. I suggested that you listen keenly to yourself; and I suggest that you look sharply at yourself. You may feel that you're going to end up like the old *Movietone News,* which used to call itself the "Eyes and Ears of the World." But believe me, you'll become one terrific understander of human nature—yours as well as other people's. This will pay all kinds of dividends and it will also help you to appreciate Ingmar Bergman movies.

By now, I guess you've caught onto the fact that all this discipline and reinforcement and determination and self-congratulation and praise and approval are the things you're going to fill your life with—instead of depression.

The key to achieving all this is your belief that you can do it.

All those yea-sayers, from Dr. Emile Coué through Dr. Norman Vincent Peale, have a point. I suspect we are approaching the time in the not too distant future when the exact connections between chemical output in the brain and thought itself will be documented. Then perhaps a certain kind of legitimacy will be granted to us yea-sayers. I can almost read the label now: "Take two tablets of affirmation after waking and before retiring." Until the precise chemical reactions are spelled out, I hope you'll take it on faith and see if it works for you.

Again, Koestler offers a useful insight in his remarkable book *The Act of Creation:*

> We are literally "poisoned" by our adrenal humours; reason has little power over irritability or anxiety; *it takes time to talk a person out of a mood* [italics are mine] however valid the arguments; passion is blind to better judgment; anger and fear show physical after-effects long after their causes have been removed. If we could change our moods as quickly as we jump from one thought to another we would be acrobats of emotion.
>
> Thinking, in its physiological aspect, is based on electro-chemical activities in the cerebral cortex and related regions of the brain, involving energy transactions which are minute compared to the massive glandular, visceral, and muscular changes that occur when emotions are aroused. These changes are governed by phylogentically much older parts of the brain than the roof-structures which enable man to think in verbal symbols. Behaviour at any moment is the outcome of complex processes which operate on several levels of the nervous system, from the spinal cord to our latest acquisition, the pre-frontal lobes. . . .

So, while thinking does affect chemical output in the brain (which in turn affects mood), it is not as strong a dose as the chemistry of feeling. Thinking can help. Thinking can work for you, but you must give it time and the opportunity to build up its positive effects—especially in the face of the Goliath, emotions, against which it must contend.

CHAPTER 22

How to Use This Book

There are a number of ways you can use this book:

As a mirror—I have hoped and wanted you to see yourself reflected, along with millions of others who suffer from our problem, to see that you can help yourself and we can help each other.

As a feather—I have wanted and hoped to tickle you with a little humor about the higher aspects of our condition, figuring that a little levity might help lift the intolerable weight of your depression.

As a pillow—I have hoped and wanted to offer a cushion for when you're flat on your back. Everybody needs to be propped up now and then, if only in order to be able to see that they still have feet to stand on.

As a down comforter—I have wanted and hoped to comfort you by sharing my down insights with you in the sincere wish that you might gain some warmth and solace from them. And most of all—

As a launching pad.

At this very moment, you are at a crossroad. By reading this far, you took a step along a path that leads toward what may be a desired but unknown goal. The one thing you can say for the path you've been traveling is that you are familiar with it, and being familiar with anything has its own comfort. But, as I've said before, it's the comfort of a bad habit.

The road ahead will very soon become comfortable too. But more important, I am truly convinced that it could lead you to a much happier life, a life in which you steadily discover more things that are enjoyable, pleasurable, and satisfying.

The only things standing in your way at this moment are: the initial reluctance of jumping into water which is a few degrees cooler than the air you're in now (but once you take the plunge, you'll find it refreshing, not frightening), and the innate laziness of the human creature—who may be willing to try something once, but is extremely reluctant to keep on trying long enough to have it work.

Not only will you have to risk going down this new road, you'll have to stay on it and continue traveling toward your goal without looking back. When I've wanted something with all my heart, I've always said, "If it would help me to get it, I'd crawl to Philadelphia on my belly!" I promise you this: if you want to be free of your depressions badly enough to crawl to Philadelphia on your belly, *you can be free of them.*

In breaking, or reorganizing, the old habit of depression (this also applies to any habit), there are three areas that have to be dealt with:

1. Your mind set—something has got to help you switch your dial from negative self-images to positive self-images (pick out whichever nostrums you think will help bring this about).
2. Your psychological/physiological established responses—you've got to wean yourself, with some discomfort, away from the ways you've been responding to stimuli that have brought about your mental and physical downs and establish new responses that help keep you on an even keel.
3. Your automatic mental responses—which have to be broken and reset like a limb that doesn't function the way you want it to.

Let's discuss how you can go about working on these areas.

We all have voices in our heads which talk to us on an almost constant basis. Our voices give us messages continually, and what they say to us affects us in every way.

If your voices tell you you are a failure, or that you're unattractive, inadequate, and don't relate well to others . . . you believe them. And you act on what you believe to be true. You act on what you believe both consciously and unconsciously. Your body and your mind act on these beliefs psychologically, physiologically, emotionally, and any other way you can name. In other words, those voices of yours dictate to a very large extent who and what you are! (As an example, you may be amused to know that my voices talk to me in a southern accent—they tell me what to write—as I am writing—and the reason I know about their southern accent is that I have caught myself making the same typographical errors repeatedly, for the simple reason that I am writing what I *hear* in my head and many of my typos are the result of spelling words the way they *sound* in my head . . . such as "kep" for "kept." I am not hearing the final 't,' so when I write fast, I only put down what I hear.) Several of my voices use other accents, however, and *what* I am writing is related to which ones have the floor.

Several times in this book I have offered "programming" tips—suggestions of things to say aloud to yourself and things to think to yourself. This is to help you program your voices to say things that will make you happy, not miserable. When I have emphasized saying things aloud, for instance, it is to drown out the inner voices, who, like people you know who don't give you a chance to get a word in, have to be shouted down. Once you establish the new habit of asserting yourself over the negative voices in your head, you'll find they aren't so hard to get past. And eventually your positive messages will assert themselves.

You *can* prevent your voices from saying destructive things.

You *can* replace the old lines with constructive new lines.

You *can* create a fine human drama out of a bad melodrama. This will take determination, dedication, discipline, and devotion—which are your "good" replacements for the list of "bad Ds."

If your voices supply the dialogue in your drama of daily living, your imagination supplies the action. You are also constantly playing scenes in your head. You live through situations that have already occurred or you project scenes that you believe may occur. You see yourself in these scenes—and, all too often, the action you create for yourself is damaging, threatening, scary, destructive, or dangerous.

Recreate the action too! Write constructive, meaningful action for the scenes you have *not yet* lived through, and examine with a keen professional eye the scenes you *have* lived through. Then extract instruction and help rather than self-beratement and depression. Remember in chapter one, when we went through the scene you played with the friend who broke the dinner date? That's what I mean about re-creating the action. You extracted all kinds of information and help when you replayed it for instruction rather than depression.

You make the most significant contribution to the creation of your own life. More than your parents, or siblings or peers, you do most of the shaping of the story. You can decide how you want it to come out. You can choose the pace at which it is played, whether it's an adventure story or a love story or a story of achievement. You can make it into a saga, if you want, and span generations within one lifetime—*if* you take hold of your own life and create it for yourself.

Lastly, talk to others who suffer from depression. If you can, offer them solace, help, and understanding. When you find nostrums of your own which work for you, I hope you will tell others about them. These will be the best nostrums of all, because they will be the ones you create for yourself.

Like Alcoholics Anonymous and Overeaters Anonymous, there should be a structure for depressives so that they can draw on each other's strength and tenderness and understanding. Perhaps you will make such an organization among your friends or acquaintances and set a time and a place to meet and share problems and solutions.

I hope you will regard *The Down Comforter* as a sort of emporium, with shelves full of colorful nostrums to choose from. I hope you will return to it when your supplies of hope or courage or determination run low—and that you will continue to find stores of what you need. This will happen if you do the replenishing yourself.

No matter where you are in life, you can bring about your own reincarnation! You can come back as a new person, without changing who you are.

Maybe you can really begin to be who you are.

The alternative is to just let it happen. If you're depressed, by doing nothing, you are effectively choosing to keep the negative.

The act of making a conscious choice is more important than *what* is chosen. There are times when you can make use of the negative factors. But only when you know what you're doing and why—when you *choose* the negative, not when you are helplessly chosen.

So after you write your script, you must rehearse your voices and guide the action. You must stop them when they miss lines or fall back into delivering the same old script. You are the playwright, the director, and the producer. You are also the backer and the angel—and since you have everything at stake, you must be a relentless taskmaster in your own production.

Anything that encourages and exercises your imagination and your creative abilities will enrich and strengthen your life. Launch yourself into a new world of self-discovery and other-discovery.

When you begin to look at the world and listen to the world, smell, touch, feel, and taste the world, you'll be discovering chords of responsiveness in yourself at the same time. It's all *out* there waiting for you, and it's all *in* there waiting for you.

One of my favorite poets, Rainer Maria Rilke, wrote:

> ... Yes, the Springs had need of you. Many a star was waiting for you to espy it. Many a wave would rise on the past towards you; or else, perhaps, as you went by an open window, a violin would be giving itself to someone. All this was a trust. But were you equal to it? Were you not always distracted by expectation as though all this were announcing someone to love? ...

Appendix: Thumbnail Sketches of Newer Psychotherapies

Here are some sketches of newer psychotherapies. Bear in mind that within each school there are many variations and off-shoots. Most important to realize in evaluating *any* psychotherapy is that it is, after all, just another kind of human relation and that the interaction between the individuals involved is the most meaningful aspect.

est (Erhard Seminars Training) is a crash course in getting you to confront yourself. Conducted in large groups under the supervision of a "trainer," est condenses the slower, longer approach of more traditional therapies in breaking down their defenses. It has (by testimony of those who have undergone it) a very powerful effect in releasing deep feelings. There is a spiritual overtone inherent in the somewhat messianic view of the message of the founder and sage, Werner Erhard. The group size runs from 200 to 250 people who are locked up together in a huge room for two successive Saturday and Sunday all-day sessions. During the lockup, no one is permitted to eat or go to the bathroom except once a day (sixteen hours). The participants sit on hard wooden chairs and are constantly harangued by a trainer on the principles of est. It cost upwards of $250. Its greatest attribute is that it can help the individual get unstuck and thereby lead to the possibility of making a dramatic reassessment of things. Est is therefore most helpful to the depressed person when it leads to *other* things. It is not the safest approach for those who feel fragile emotionally, since it is designed to disturb or otherwise shake you up.

Primal Screaming—or primal therapy—was invented by Arthur Janov when, by chance, a patient's reaction to an off-the-cuff suggestion of Janov's led to a breakthrough into an area of real feeling which he had not been in touch with before. Janov experimented and finally formulated a system which is based on the idea that the parent did something (withheld love, most often) which hurt the child and laid the groundwork for the neurosis. Primal scream-ing affords the patient the opportunity to literally scream out the pain and, in so doing, to exorcise it. During an intensified period of three weeks, the patient does nothing but undergo treatment and the therapist treats only the one patient. Each session (which lasts as long as the therapist deems wise) has a specific goal which is related to the early parent-child trauma—and never to anything extraneous to that problem. This technique allows for the flushing out of long-buried and toxic feelings which have acted destructively on the individual since childhood. The objective is to free the real self from these encrustations. It is a highly charged emotional experience, which has something in common with est and with revivalist religions. It is also not to be advised for fragile-feeling periods of your life. This therapy is particularly prone to abuse by charlatan types.

Bioenergetics are a group of therapies all working on the principle that the basic matter to be considered in seeking emotional health is the body, not the mind. A number of proponents, including Wilhelm Reich, F. S. Alexander, Ida Rolf, and Moshe Feldenkrais, have worked from this thesis. The verbal and the social intercourse aspects are very much played down. It's not so much what people say, goes the theory, as what they do with their bodies to express what's going on inside them. Therefore, part of the treatment is the manipulation of the body by encouraging the expression of feelings physically and the actual laying on of hands to help the individual release tension and freely express feelings and desires. There is a tie-in, of course, with sexuality, and the main criterion of health is the ability of the individual to reach orgasm with a member of the opposite sex. (Alone or with someone of the same sex is no good.)

Rogerian Therapy, named after Carl Rogers, is one of the "humanistic" therapies. This group, which includes bioenergetics, aims to break down barriers, to keep options open, to pursue wholeness through direct experience. The humanistic therapies are more concerned with unhappiness and alienation than with neurosis or psychosis. Rogerian therapy in particular concentrates on improving the individual's quality of life. It is the *whole* person which is to be dealt with. *Positivism* is the key word, and it operates within the individual's personal or subjective evaluation of him/herself and what he/she feels to be subjectively real and valuable. Like the other humanistic approaches, Rogerian therapy is an American development in psychology, and the pragmatic is emphasized. The Rogerian therapist regards the patient as a "client" and functions as a reflecting surface in which the client can see him/herself as a well-regarded human being, who is worthwhile because he/she *is*. Rogerians believe in the essential goodness of the human being, and the accent is on bringing out the good self-images as opposed to the bad self-images. It is basically an educational and socializational process, and has had a great deal of influence in those fields.

Gestalt Therapy puts more emphasis on feeling than on thinking. Nonverbal experience is more important than verbal, just as the body is more important than the mind. In fact, the idea is to eliminate the disjunction between the mind and the body. Frederick (Fritz) Perls, who had training in Freudian analysis, is the chief founder of Gestalt therapy. The Gestalt therapist believes that the whole person (the organism) must function as part of nature. Perls argues that the organism knows and wants this relationship (is conscious or aware of an innate drive to achieve it) and strives toward fulfilling that natural integration. The patient is encouraged to express all needs, desires, angers, and resentments openly—not so much in word, but in body movements, tone of voice, posture, and so forth. Gestalt fosters a group session approach where the sessions are a part of a total living experience for short periods of time. Instead of talking out problems and conflicts, the Gestalt acts them out, playing different roles or parts at different times. The patient may shift back and forth, playing different segments of her/himself—different aspects of his/her personality (the bully, the underdog, etc.)—and by so doing, comes to realize that all of the various parts are part of his/her organism. One of the many American forms of Eastern religion, Gestalt therapy fosters intense emotional experiences in a group setting. These experiences can become so heightened as to approach hysteria. There is a relationship to the possession states of the shamanistic experience.

Psychodrama is the brainchild of J. L. Moreno. Acting out is literal, in that actual roles are set up from real social contexts. And since each person plays many different roles in reality—boss, worker, lover, spouse, friend, sibling, hero, patsy, success, failure, achiever, dilettante—each person uses the different roles to portray the actuality of his/her current life. Where there are conflicts, the individual will play the conflicting or contradictory roles in turn. This enables the patient to view the entire situation from various vantage points and to see all the angles, finally arriving at an integrated overview of the whole picture in which he/she is involved. The therapist is the "director" and guides the action while interacting with the group and the leading character. The rest of the group identifies with the protagonist and the situation while it is going on. After the dramatic presentation, there is usually a discussion of the feelings and the situation of the scenario as related to "real" life.

Transactional Analysis is the "I'm O.K.—You're O.K." therapy which swept the country in the wake of Dr. Thomas Harris's book of the same name. The originator, Eric Berne—who also wrote a highly popular bestseller, *Games People Play*—was trained in Freudian analysis, but went into group therapy and developed his ideas for transactional analysis (or TA, as it is referred to) while working with members of the group and observing their interactions—which he called transactions. TA is concerned with attitudes toward the self—security or insecurity feelings, self-esteem, inferiority—which are either "Okay" or "Not Okay." Those attitudes have to do with how a person behaves more than whatever the deep-rooted causes of his/her neurosis might be. TA describes three "ego states," which alternate within the individual: the Parent, the Adult, and the Child. There is a lot of interplay within the group, and everybody analyzes everybody else's "games" or "transactions" to discern the patterns that have made the person "Okay" or "Not Okay" all his/her life. The goal is to give the Adult ego state control over the Parent and the Child. This approach is a practical way of emphasizing and promoting the individual's ability to get along in the world. TA is a short-term course of group sessions which meet once a week for roughly ten weeks. The course of meetings can be repeated.

Behavioral-Directive Therapies are fundamentally committed to the idea that the individual's essential problem can be observed in his/her behavior. It is something the person *does*, not something the person *is*. The treatment, therefore, is to help the individual adjust the behavior. "Sex therapy" is a prominent example in which the problem is located and dealt with in a specific form of behavior alteration. In all directive therapies, the therapist offers suggestions for ways in which to change or correct faulty behavior. Hypnosis is one means, and Dr. William Glasser's "reality therapy"—which says that if you behave properly, your problems will clear up—is another. Behavior-directive therapies are very popular, and there are many variations and techniques for helping the individual to overcome a specific behavioral problem. Joseph Wolpe, for instance, employs what is called systematic desensitization to overcome specific phobias. B. F. Skinner's approach, "operant conditioning," is used a great deal in institutions in the attempt to modify the behavior of social outcasts.